GRADE 3

P9-AGN-960

MATH Trailblazers

A BALANCED MATHEMATICS PROGRAM INTEGRATING SCIENCE AND LANGUAGE ARTS

Unit Resource Guide
Unit 5

Area of
Different Shapes

THIRD EDITION

KENDALL/HUNT PUBLISHING COMPANY
4050 Westmark Drive   Dubuque, Iowa 52002

A TIMS® Curriculum
University of Illinois at Chicago

UIC The University of Illinois
at Chicago

The original edition was based on work supported by the National Science Foundation under grant No. MDR 9050226 and the University of Illinois at Chicago. Any opinions, findings, and conclusions or recommendations expressed in this publication are those of the author(s) and do not necessarily reflect the views of the granting agencies.

Letter Home

Area of Different Shapes

Date: _____

Dear Family Member:

Area is the amount of surface needed to cover something—the amount of carpet to cover a floor, wallpaper to cover a wall, or skin to cover a body. In this next unit, your child will explore the area of flat surfaces.

We will find the area of shapes that have straight, curved, or irregular sides, such as the shape shown here. To find the area of an irregular shape, students trace the shape on centimeter grid paper. They first count the number of full centimeter squares inside the shape. Then they piece together the remaining parts (for example, halves) into full squares. This gives a good estimate of the shape's area. The class will apply its knowledge of area to an experiment that investigates which brand of paper towels absorbs the most water.

As we study area in our classroom, you can help reinforce the concept of area at home with the following activities.

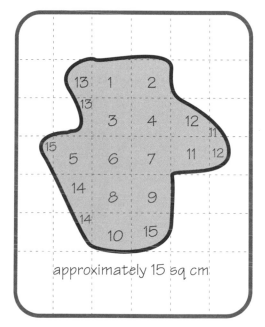

approximately 15 sq cm

Counting the number of square centimeters in a shape to find area

- **Measure Your Handprint's Area.** Have different members of your family trace their handprints on a piece of paper and ask your child to compare the area of each by covering them with pennies or beans. Compare the area of your handprints with the area of your footprints. Which has more area?
- **Shape Tracings.** Help your child look for different shapes around the house, such as a plate or leaf. Trace the shapes on paper. Ask your child to compare the area of the different shapes by covering them with pennies or beans.
- **Math Facts.** Help your child study the subtraction facts in Groups 7 and 8 using flash cards.

Thank you for taking time to do math at home with your child. It helps your child connect mathematics to everyday experiences.

Sincerely,

_____

Carta al hogar

El área de diferentes figuras

Fecha: _____

Estimado miembro de familia:

El área es la cantidad de superficie necesaria para cubrir algo, como la cantidad de alfombra necesaria para cubrir un piso, papel tapiz para cubrir una pared o piel para cubrir un cuerpo. En esta unidad, su hijo/a explorará el área de superficies planas.

Hallaremos el área de figuras que tienen lados rectos, curvos o irregulares, como la que se muestra aquí. Para hallar el área de una figura irregular, los estudiantes calcan la figura en papel con cuadrículas de un centímetro. Primero cuentan los cuadrados de un centímetro llenos dentro de la figura. Luego juntan las partes restantes (por ejemplo, mitades) en cuadrados completos. Esto les permite hacer una buena estimación del área de la figura. La clase aplicará el conocimiento sobre el área en un experimento en el cuál se investigar qué marca de toallas de papel absorbe mayor cantidad de agua.

Mientras estudiamos el área en clase, usted puede ayudar a reforzar este concepto en casa haciendo las siguientes actividades.

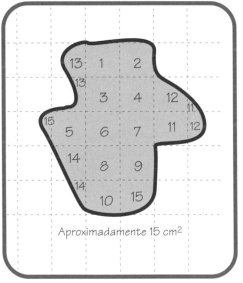

Aproximadamente 15 cm²

Contar el número de centímetros cuadrados en una figura para hallar el área.

- **Medir el área de la huella de la mano.** Haga que varios miembros de la familia calquen las huellas de sus manos en una hoja de papel y pídale a su hijo/a que compare el área de cada una cubriéndolas con monedas de un centavo o frijoles. Compare el área de las huellas de sus manos con el área de las huellas de sus pies. ¿Cuál es mayor?
- **Calcar figuras.** Ayude a su hijo/a a buscar distintas figuras en la casa, tales como un plato o la hoja de una planta. Calque las figuras en papel. Pídale a su hijo/a que compare el área de las diferentes figuras cubriéndolas con monedas de un centavo o frijoles.
- **Conceptos básicos.** Ayude a su hijo/a a estudiar las restas básicas de los grupos 7 y 8 usando tarjetas.

Gracias por tomarse el tiempo para practicar matemáticas con su hijo/a en casa. Esto ayuda a su hijo/a a relacionar las matemáticas con experiencias cotidianas.

Atentamente,

Table of Contents

Unit 5
Area of Different Shapes

Unit 5

Outline
Area of Different Shapes

Unit Summary

Estimated Class Sessions
8-10

Students' concept of area is strengthened through a series of activities where they find the area of irregular shapes by counting square centimeters. In the introductory activity, students piece together fractional parts of square centimeters into full units. In the experiment *The Better "Picker Upper,"* students apply this skill toward understanding which of several brands of paper towel is the best for soaking up water. The lab also provides a context for problem solving and for a discussion of the roles of fixed (controlled) variables in experiments. Students read the Adventure Book *The Haunted House,* a story about a team of amateur detectives who solve a mystery by measuring the area of a ghost's footprint. The DPP for this unit review the subtraction facts for Groups 7 and 8 and develop multiplication facts strategies for the square numbers.

Major Concept Focus

- TIMS Laboratory Method
- bar graphs
- median
- fixed variables
- area of irregular shapes
- measuring area in square centimeters
- counting halves and fourths of square centimeters
- relationship between shape and area
- using multiplication
- *Adventure Book:* area
- Student Rubric: *Solving*
- assessing problem solving
- subtraction facts review for Groups 7 and 8
- multiplication facts strategies for the square numbers

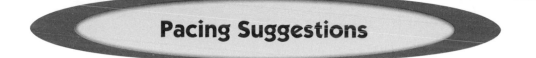

Pacing Suggestions

- Lesson 3 *The Better "Picker Upper"* provides connections to science. Students can collect the data for the lab during science time.
- Lesson 4 *The Haunted House* is an *Adventure Book* story that provides a connection to language arts. Students can read the story as part of language arts time.
- Lesson 6 *Using Number Sense at the Book Sale* is an optional lesson. It is a series of word problems that provides practice with money.

Assessment Indicators

Use the following Assessment Indicators and the *Observational Assessment Record* that follows the Background section in this unit to assess students on key ideas.

A1. Can students find the area of shapes with straight or curved sides by counting square units?

A2. Do students recognize that different shapes can have the same area?

A3. Can students find the median of a data set?

A4. Can students identify and use variables?

A5. Can students make and interpret bar graphs?

A6. Can students collect, organize, graph, and analyze data?

A7. Can students use data to make predictions and solve problems?

A8. Can students solve open-response problems and communicate solution strategies?

Unit Planner

	Lesson Information	Supplies	Copies/Transparencies
Lesson 1 **Measuring Area** URG Pages 20–30 SG Pages 58–59 DAB Page 87 DPP A–B *Estimated Class Sessions* **1**	**Activity** Students find the area of an irregular shape by helping Professor Peabody find the number of tiles he will need to cover a floor. They also find the area of other polygons and curved shapes. **Math Facts** For DPP Bit A, students practice the subtraction facts in Group 7. **Homework** Assign the *Area of Five Shapes* Homework Page.		• 1 transparency of *Centimeter Grid Paper* URG Page 28, optional
Lesson 2 **Boo the Blob** URG Pages 31–38 DAB Pages 89–91 DPP C–D HP Parts 1–2 *Estimated Class Sessions* **1**	**Activity** Students investigate the relationship between shape and area and estimate the area of irregular shapes. They also learn to find the median value of data. **Math Facts** DPP Bit C introduces the *Subtraction Flash Cards: Group 7.* **Homework** 1. Students use their flash cards at home to study the subtraction facts in Group 7. 2. Assign Home Practice Parts 1 and 2. **Assessment** Observe students finding the area of irregular shapes and comparing different shapes with the same area while completing the *Boo the Blob Changes Shape* Activity Pages. Record observations on the *Observational Assessment Record.*	• 1 pair of scissors per student • 1 envelope per student for storing flash cards	• 1 copy of *Centimeter Grid Paper* URG Page 28 per student • 1 copy of *Observational Assessment Record* URG Pages 9–10 to be used throughout this unit
Lesson 3 **The Better "Picker Upper"** URG Pages 39–58 SG Pages 60–61 DAB Pages 93–98 DPP E–L HP Part 3 *Estimated Class Sessions* **4-5**	**Lab** Students investigate the area of a spot made by a given number of drops of water on different brands of paper towels. They measure the area of the spots by counting square units. They use this information to decide which brand is most absorbent. **Math Facts** DPP Tasks H and J are multiplication problems. DPP Bits I and K work with the subtraction facts in Group 8. **Homework** 1. Students use their flash cards at home to study the subtraction facts in Group 8. 2. Assign *Lori's Questions* Homework Pages. **Assessment** 1. The lab provides opportunities to observe the many aspects of conducting a lab. Use the *Observational Assessment Record* to record students' abilities to measure area and organize data.	• 1 eyedropper per student group • 3–4 brands of paper towels of varying quality, one sheet of each brand per student group • 1 pair of scissors per student group • 1 small container of water per student group • 2 books or 1 geoboard for drying paper towels per student group	• 1 copy of *Centimeter Grid Paper* URG Page 28 per student • 1 copy of *Centimeter Graph Paper* URG Page 53 per student • 1 transparency of *Centimeter Graph Paper* URG Page 53

	Lesson Information	Supplies	Copies/ Transparencies
	2. Use *Questions 3* and *4* of the *Lori's Questions* Homework Pages to evaluate students' abilities to find the area of irregular shapes.	• 1 envelope per student for storing flash cards • food coloring, optional	
Lesson 4 **The Haunted House** URG Pages 59–66 AB Pages 26–42 DPP M–N HP Part 4 *Estimated Class Sessions* **1**	**Adventure Book** Rosita and Peter solve a mystery about a haunted house by measuring the area and length of a "ghost's" footprints. **Homework** For Home Practice Part 4, students solve multiplication problems using square numbers.		
Lesson 5 **Joe the Goldfish** URG Pages 67–76 DPP O–P *Estimated Class Sessions* **1**	**Assessment Activity** Students work in pairs or groups to determine the amount of material it would take to make a raincoat for Joe the Goldfish. They design the coat and determine its area in square centimeters. Students are introduced to the Student Rubric: *Solving.* **Math Facts** DPP items O and P practice math facts. **Assessment** 1. Document students' abilities to solve open-response problems and communicate solution strategies using the *Observational Assessment Record.* 2. Use the Unit 5 *Observational Assessment Record* to update students' *Individual Assessment Record Sheets.*	• 1 pair of scissors per student group	• 1 copy of *A Raincoat for Joe the Goldfish* URG Page 75 per student • 1 copy of *Centimeter Grid Paper* URG Page 28 per student group • 1 transparency of *A Raincoat for Joe the Goldfish* URG Page 75, optional • 1 transparency of *Centimeter Grid Paper* URG Page 28, optional • 1 copy of *Individual Assessment Record Sheet* TIG Assessment section per student, previously copied for use throughout the year
Lesson 6 **Using Number Sense at the Book Sale** URG Pages 77–81 SG Pages 62–64 *Estimated Class Sessions* **1**	OPTIONAL LESSON **Optional Activity** Students solve word problems from a list of books and prices. **Homework** Assign some or all of the problems for homework.		

Preparing for Upcoming Lessons

Place eyedroppers in a learning center for students to explore prior to Lesson 3. You may want to introduce eyedroppers in a whole class setting.

You will need to purchase three different brands of paper towels for Lesson 3.

Connections

A current list of literature and software connections is available at *www.mathtrailblazers.com*. You can also find information on connections in the *Teacher Implementation Guide* Literature List and Software List sections.

Literature Connections

Suggested Titles

- Gabriel, Nat. *Sam's Sneaker Squares.* The Kane Press, New York, 2002.
- Murphy, Stuart J. *Room for Ripley.* HarperCollins Publishing, New York, 1999.

Software Connections

- *The Factory Deluxe* promotes spatial reasoning and practices finding area.
- *Graphers* is a data graphing tool appropriate for young students.
- *Kid Pix* allows students to create their own illustrations.
- *National Library of Virtual Manipulatives* website (http://matti.usu.edu) allows students to work with manipulatives including geoboards, base-ten pieces, the abacus, and many others.

Teaching All Math Trailblazers Students

Math Trailblazers® lessons are designed for students with a wide range of abilities. The lessons are flexible and do not require significant adaptation for diverse learning styles or academic levels. However, when needed, lessons can be tailored to allow students to engage their abilities to the greatest extent possible while building knowledge and skills.

To assist you in meeting the needs of all students in your classroom, this section contains information about some of the features in the curriculum that allow all students access to mathematics. For additional information, see the Teaching the *Math Trailblazers* Student: Meeting Individual Needs section in the *Teacher Implementation Guide*.

Differentiation Opportunities in this Unit

Laboratory Experiments

Laboratory experiments enable students to solve problems using a variety of representations including pictures, tables, graphs, and symbols. Teachers can assign or adapt parts of the analysis according to the student's ability. The following lesson is a lab:

- Lesson 3 *The Better "Picker Upper"*

Journal Prompts

Journal prompts provide opportunities for students to explain and reflect on mathematical problems. They can help both students who need practice explaining their ideas and students who benefit from answering higher order questions. Students with various learning styles can express themselves using pictures, words, and sentences. Teachers can alter journal prompts to suit students' ability levels. The following lessons contain a journal prompt:

- Lesson 3 *The Better "Picker Upper"*
- Lesson 4 *The Haunted House*
- Lesson 5 *Joe the Goldfish*

DPP Challenges

DPP Challenges are items from the Daily Practice and Problems that usually take more than fifteen minutes to complete. These problems are more thought-provoking and can be used to stretch students' problem-solving skills. The following lessons have a DPP Challenge in them:

- DPP Challenge B from Lesson 1 *Measuring Area*
- DPP Challenge L from Lesson 3 *The Better "Picker Upper"*

Extensions

Use extensions to enrich lessons. Many extensions provide opportunities to further involve or challenge students of all abilities. Take a moment to review the extensions prior to beginning this unit. Some extensions may require additional preparation and planning. The following lessons contain extensions:

- Lesson 2 *Boo the Blob*
- Lesson 3 *The Better "Picker Upper"*
- Lesson 4 *The Haunted House*
- Lesson 6 *Using Number Sense at the Book Sale*

Background
Area of Different Shapes

Area is the amount of surface needed to cover something—the amount of carpet to cover a floor, wallpaper to cover a wall, or skin to cover a body. Area is measured in square units, such as square inches or square meters. For example, ecologists measure the amount of rain forest destroyed each day in square miles. Neurobiologists measure the area of individual connections between nerve cells in square microns. (One square micron is $\frac{1}{100,000,000}$ of a square centimeter.)

In third grade, students find the area of flat surfaces. Building on the ideas they developed in first and second grades, they begin this unit by finding the area of shapes with straight sides. Then, they learn to measure the area of shapes with curved sides. The activities and experiment in this unit provide a context in which to develop a working definition of area by counting square units.

Students face a series of problems that cannot be solved by measuring length or width, but only by measuring area:

- How many tiles will it take to cover a floor?
- Can two or more different shapes have the same area?

- Can two amateur detectives identify a class-mate by measuring the area of a footprint?
- How much material will it take to make a raincoat?

In the lab in Lesson 3 *The Better "Picker Upper,"* students decide which of several brands of paper towels is the most absorbent. The lab allows students to use their knowledge of area and the scientific process to explore many facets of a problem. They identify the variables in the experiment and collect, record, and graph data. Students identify the most absorbent towel by interpreting the graph and answering the questions posed in the lab.

Developing a conceptual understanding of area in the primary grades gives students information they need to solve problems similar to those in this unit. It also provides the framework for more advanced work with area in mathematics and science, such as finding the surface area of three-dimensional figures. For more information, refer to the TIMS Tutor: *The Concept of Area* in the *Teacher Implementation Guide.*

Observational Assessment Record

A1 Can students find the area of shapes with straight or curved sides by counting square units?

A2 Do students recognize that different shapes can have the same area?

A3 Can students find the median of a data set?

A4 Can students identify and use variables?

A5 Can students make and interpret bar graphs?

A6 Can students collect, organize, graph, and analyze data?

A7 Can students use data to make predictions and solve problems?

A8 Can students solve open-response problems and communicate solution strategies?

A9 _____

Name	A1	A2	A3	A4	A5	A6	A7	A8	A9	Comments
1.										
2.										
3.										
4.										
5.										
6.										
7.										
8.										
9.										
10.										
11.										
12.										

Name	A1	A2	A3	A4	A5	A6	A7	A8	A9	Comments
13										
14.										
15.										
16.										
17.										
18.										
19.										
20.										
21.										
22.										
23.										
24.										
25.										
26.										
27.										
28.										
29.										
30.										
31.										
32.										

Unit 5

Daily Practice and Problems
Area of Different Shapes

A DPP Menu for Unit 5

Two Daily Practice and Problems (DPP) items are included for each class session listed in the Unit Outline. A scope and sequence chart for the DPP is in the *Teacher Implementation Guide*.

Icons in the Teacher Notes column designate the subject matter of each DPP item. The first item in each class session is always a Bit and the second is either a Task or Challenge. Each item falls into one or more of the categories listed below. A menu of the DPP items for Unit 5 follows.

N Number Sense	Computation	Time	Geometry
D–G	B, L, N		M

Math Facts	$ Money	Measurement	Data
A, C, H–K, O, P	H	M	E, G

Practicing the Subtraction Facts

DPP items in this unit provide review of the subtraction facts for Group 7 ($14 - 7$, $14 - 6$, $14 - 8$, $12 - 6$, $12 - 7$, $12 - 5$, $10 - 5$, $13 - 7$, $13 - 6$) and Group 8 ($15 - 7$, $16 - 8$, $17 - 8$, $18 - 9$, $18 - 10$, $8 - 4$, $7 - 4$, $6 - 3$, $15 - 8$). Students can solve facts in these groups by using doubles and reasoning from related addition facts (thinking addition).

DPP items C and K ask students to use flash cards to study these subtraction facts and update their *Subtraction Facts I Know* charts. *Subtraction Flash Cards: Groups 7* and *8* are in the *Discovery Assignment Book* following the Home Practice. See DPP items A, I, and O for practice with these facts.

Developing Strategies for the Multiplication Facts

DPP items in this unit develop strategies for the multiplication facts for square numbers. See DPP items H, J, and P for work with square numbers.

For information on the practice and assessment of subtraction facts in Grade 3, see the Lesson Guide for Unit 2 Lesson 7 *Assessing the Subtraction Facts.* For information on the study of the multiplication facts in Grade 3, see the DPP Guide for Unit 11. For a detailed explanation of our approach to learning and assessing the math facts in Grade 3, see the *Grade 3 Facts Resource Guide,* and for information for Grades K–5, see the TIMS Tutor: *Math Facts* in the *Teacher Implementation Guide.*

 **Daily Practice and Problems**

Students may solve the items individually, in groups, or as a class. The items may also be assigned for homework. The DPPs are also available on the Teacher Resource CD.

Student Questions	Teacher Notes

A **Subtraction: Using Doubles**

Do these problems in your head. Write only the answers.

1. $14 - 7 =$

2. $14 - 6 =$

3. $14 - 8 =$

4. $12 - 6 =$

5. $12 - 7 =$

6. $12 - 5 =$

7. $100 - 50 =$

8. $13 - 7 =$

9. $13 - 6=$

10. Explain your strategy for solving Question 6.

TIMS Bit

This bit corresponds to *Subtraction Flash Cards: Group 7*. Students are usually quite comfortable with addition "doubles." They can solve the facts in this group by "thinking addition" with doubles. ($14 - 7 = 7$ because $7 + 7 = 14$) Students can also use doubles to figure out "near doubles" such as $14 - 6 = 8$.

1. 7
2. 8
3. 6
4. 6
5. 5
6. 7
7. 50
8. 6
9. 7
10. Possible strategy: Students can use the subtraction fact $12 - 6 = 6$ to reason that $12 - 5$ will be one more or 7 ($12 - 5 = 7$).

Student Questions	Teacher Notes

B · Pancakes for Breakfast

Fifteen Girl Scouts are planning an overnight camping trip. Two mothers will also go. They are planning to have dollar-sized pancakes and sausages for breakfast.

Each scout plans to eat 10 pancakes and 3 sausages. Each mother plans to eat 5 pancakes and 2 sausages. How many pancakes and sausages will they need?

TIMS Challenge

One possible strategy:

Students can use skip counting either on the calculator or with pencil and paper.

Pancakes for scouts:	150
Pancakes for mothers:	10
Total pancakes:	160
Sausages for scouts:	45
Sausages for mothers:	4
Total sausages:	49

C · Subtraction Flash Cards: Group 7

1. With a partner, sort the flash cards into three stacks: Facts I Know Quickly, Facts I Know Using a Strategy, and Facts I Need to Learn.

2. Update your *Subtraction Facts I Know* chart. Circle the facts you answered quickly. Underline those you knew by using a strategy. Do nothing to those you still need to learn.

TIMS Bit

Students cut out the *Subtraction Flash Cards: Group 7*. The flash cards are in the *Discovery Assignment Book* following the Home Practice. After students sort the flash cards, they should update the *Subtraction Facts I Know* chart. Students take the cards for Group 7 home to practice with their families.

D Comics

On an average day in the United States, 890 copies of a certain comic book series are sold. The number 890 is . . .

A. 10 more than ———

B. 10 less than ———

C. 100 more than ———

D. 100 less than ———

E. about half of ———

F. about twice ———

G. 800 + ———

H. 10 × ———

I. 500 + ———

J. 110 less than ———

TIMS Task [N]

After students write down their answers, let them discuss their strategies and their answers, in groups or as a class.

A. 880

B. 900

C. 790

D. 990

E. 1800

F. 450

(Answers may vary for E and F.)

G. 90

H. 89

I. 390

J. 1000

E Averaging Data

Julie did a study of candy color. Here is her data. Find the median number of candies for each color. The first one is done for you.

C Color	N Number			
	Sample 1	Sample 2	Sample 3	Median
red	3	5	4	4
brown	11	10	13	
orange	5	1	4	
green	5	6	5	

TIMS Bit [N] [/]

The rest of the medians, from top to bottom, are 11, 4, and 5.

Students will find the median values for data collected in Lesson 2 *Boo the Blob*. You may wish to use this item before students collect the data for this activity.

F More Comics

On an average day in the United States, 1096 copies of a certain comic book series are sold.

Show this number with base-ten pieces.

Show this number with base-ten shorthand.

TIMS Task

After students have worked with base-ten pieces, discuss the different ways they represented the number. Then, ask students to represent the number using the Fewest Pieces Rule.

1 pack, 9 skinnies, and 6 bits

⌷ ||||| ꞉ ꞏ ꞏ ꞏ ꞏ
       ||||

G Averaging

In an experiment, Franco measured the area of different types of leaves. Here is his data. Find the median area for each type of leaf.

T	A Area in sq cm			
Type of Leaf	Trial 1	Trial 2	Trial 3	Median
Oak	48 sq cm	55 sq cm	50 sq cm	
Maple	86 sq cm	80 sq cm	84 sq cm	
Birch	10 sq cm	10 sq cm	12 sq cm	

TIMS Bit

This is a review for finding the median. Students will need to find the median of three numbers to complete the data table in the experiment *The Better "Picker Upper."*

Leaf Type	Median
Oak	50 sq cm
Maple	84 sq cm
Birch	10 sq cm

H Kim's Savings

1. Kim earns $7 each week mowing lawns. She wants to buy jeans that cost $45. The tax will be $3. How long will she have to save to buy the jeans?

   Will she have to save longer than a month?

2. Leila earns $10 each week babysitting. How much money will she earn in 10 weeks?

TIMS Task

1. Kim will have to save for 7 weeks, which is longer than a month.

One possible strategy for solving this problem is to skip count by sevens:

Weeks:

1	2	3	4	5	6	7
$7	$14	$21	$28	$35	$42	$49

2. $100

I Subtraction: Using Doubles

Do these problems in your head. Write only the answers.

1. $16 - 8 =$ 2. $17 - 8 =$

3. $15 - 8 =$ 4. $18 - 9 =$

5. $18 - 10 =$ 6. $15 - 7 =$

7. $8 - 4 =$ 8. $7 - 4 =$

9. $60 - 30 =$

10. Explain your strategy for solving Question 4.

TIMS Bit

This bit reviews the facts in Group 8 of the *Subtraction Flash Cards*. Students can solve them by "thinking addition" using doubles, although other strategies would be as useful. Let students tell the class how they found the answers. Discuss which strategies are most efficient.

1. 8   2. 9

3. 7   4. 9

5. 8   6. 8

7. 4   8. 3

9. 30

10. Possible strategy: Students may use the addition double $9 + 9$.

Student Questions	Teacher Notes
J **Story Solving** $8 \times 8 = ?$ Write a story and draw a picture about 8×8. Write a number sentence on your picture.	**TIMS Task** Students may wish to share their stories with the class.
K **Subtraction Flash Cards: Group 8** 1. With a partner, sort the flash cards into three stacks: Facts I Know Quickly, Facts I Know Using a Strategy, and Facts I Need to Learn. 2. Update your *Subtraction Facts I Know* chart. Circle the facts you answered quickly. Underline those you knew by using a strategy. Do nothing to those you still need to learn.	**TIMS Bit** Students cut out *Subtraction Flash Cards: Group 8.* After sorting the flash cards, they should update the *Subtraction Facts I Know* chart. Have students take the cards for Groups 7 and 8 home to practice with their families.

Student Questions	Teacher Notes

L Magic Square: Sum = 27

Complete the magic square using the numbers 5, 6, 7, 8, 9, 10, 11, 12, and 13. Each row, column, and diagonal must have a sum of 27.

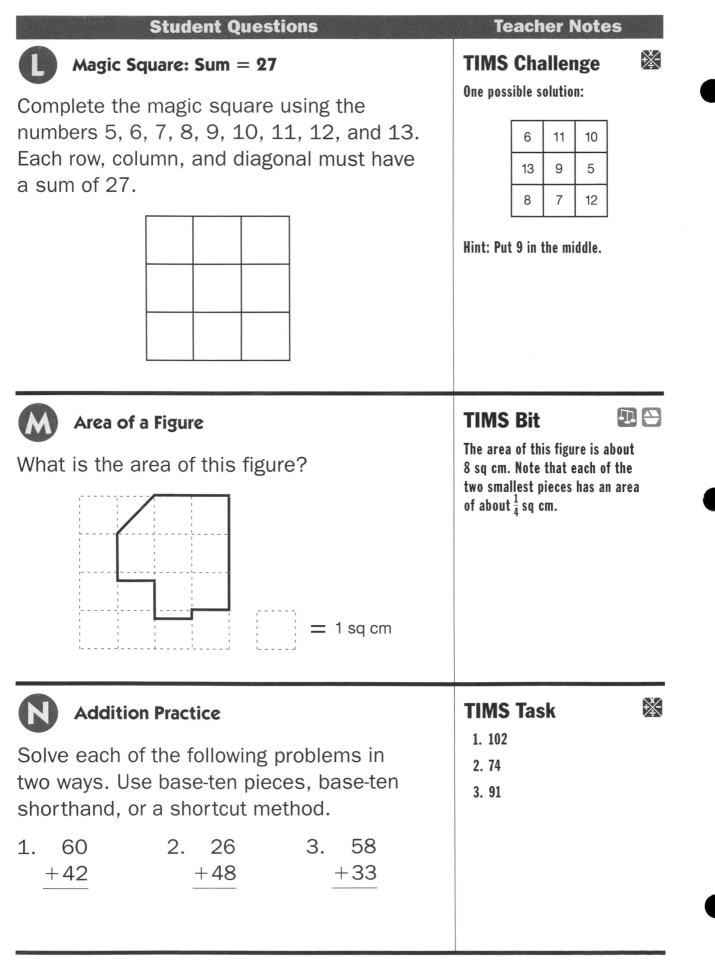

TIMS Challenge

One possible solution:

6	11	10
13	9	5
8	7	12

Hint: Put 9 in the middle.

M Area of a Figure

What is the area of this figure?

□ = 1 sq cm

TIMS Bit

The area of this figure is about 8 sq cm. Note that each of the two smallest pieces has an area of about $\frac{1}{4}$ sq cm.

N Addition Practice

Solve each of the following problems in two ways. Use base-ten pieces, base-ten shorthand, or a shortcut method.

1. 60
   +42

2. 26
   +48

3. 58
   +33

TIMS Task

1. 102
2. 74
3. 91

Student Questions	Teacher Notes

⊙ Subtraction: Strategies

Do these problems in your head. Write only the answers.

1. $15 - 7 =$

2. $11 - 6 =$

3. $14 - 6 =$

4. $13 - 4 =$

5. $11 - 3 =$

6. $17 - 8 =$

7. $16 - 7 =$

8. $13 - 8 =$

9. $17 - 9 =$

Update your *Subtraction Facts I Know* chart.

TIMS Bit ⬛ $\frac{5}{\times 7}$

This set of subtraction facts problems is taken from all the groups of subtraction facts. Students can use a variety of strategies to learn them. In a class discussion, compare strategies; is one more efficient than another?

1. 8
2. 5
3. 8
4. 9
5. 8
6. 9
7. 9
8. 5
9. 8

Ⓟ More Story Solving

$9 \times 9 = ?$ Write a story and draw a picture about 9×9.

Write a number sentence on your picture.

TIMS Task ⬛ $\frac{5}{\times 7}$

Students may wish to share their stories with the class.

Lesson 1

Measuring Area

Lesson Overview

Estimated Class Sessions

1

Students expand their understanding of area by measuring the area of irregular shapes. They count whole square units and piece together the remaining fractional ones. In this lesson, Professor Peabody is covering his living room and hall with square tiles. Students help him determine how many tiles he will need. Then, they also find the area of other polygons and curved shapes.

Key Content

- Measuring area by counting square centimeters.
- Finding the area of irregular shapes.
- Solving problems involving area.

Key Vocabulary

- area
- estimate
- square centimeter

Math Facts

For DPP Bit A, students practice the subtraction facts in Group 7.

Homework

Assign the *Area of Five Shapes* Homework Page.

Curriculum Sequence

Before This Unit

Measuring Area

In Grade 1 Unit 10 students used both nonstandard units and square inches to measure area. In Grade 2 Unit 16 students measured area by counting square centimeters and fractions of square centimeters on a grid.

After This Unit

Measuring Area

In Grade 4 Unit 2 students will review finding area by counting square units. In Grade 4 Unit 16 students will investigate the relationship between the area and length of rectangles. In Grade 5 Units 4 and 15 students will develop and use formulas for finding the areas of rectangles and triangles.

Materials List

Supplies and Copies

Student	Teacher
Supplies for Each Student	**Supplies**
Copies	**Copies/Transparencies** • 1 transparency of *Centimeter Grid Paper,* optional (*Unit Resource Guide* Page 28)

All blackline masters including assessment, transparency, and DPP masters are also on the Teacher Resource CD.

Student Books

Measuring Area (*Student Guide* Pages 58–59)
Area of Five Shapes (*Discovery Assignment Book* Page 87)

Daily Practice and Problems and Home Practice

DPP items A–B (*Unit Resource Guide* Pages 12–13)

Note: Classrooms whose pacing differs significantly from the suggested pacing of the units should use the Math Facts Calendar in Section 4 of the *Facts Resource Guide* to ensure students receive the complete math facts program.

Daily Practice and Problems

Suggestions for using the DPPs are on page 26.

A. Bit: Subtraction: Using Doubles
(URG p. 12)

Do these problems in your head. Write only the answers.

1. $14 - 7 =$
2. $14 - 6 =$
3. $14 - 8 =$
4. $12 - 6 =$
5. $12 - 7 =$
6. $12 - 5 =$
7. $100 - 50 =$
8. $13 - 7 =$
9. $13 - 6 =$
10. Explain your strategy for solving Question 6.

B. Challenge: Pancakes for Breakfast
(URG p. 13)

Fifteen Girl Scouts are planning an overnight camping trip. Two mothers will also go. They are planning to have dollar-sized pancakes and sausages for breakfast.

Each scout plans to eat 10 pancakes and 3 sausages. Each mother plans to eat 5 pancakes and 2 sausages. How many pancakes and sausages will they need?

Measuring Area

What is area?

Area is a measurement of size. We measure the area of a floor to find the amount of carpet needed to cover the floor. We can also use area to measure the amount of paper needed to wrap a present.

Area is the amount of surface that is needed to cover something. To measure the area of a shape, we tell the number of squares needed to cover the shape.

Professor Peabody has started to cover his living room and hall with square tiles. The living room is in the shape of an octagon. The hall is a rectangle.

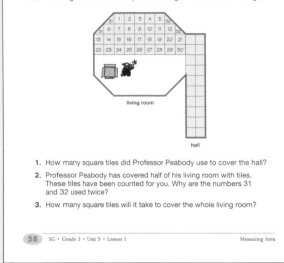

1. How many square tiles did Professor Peabody use to cover the hall?

2. Professor Peabody has covered half of his living room with tiles. These tiles have been counted for you. Why are the numbers 31 and 32 used twice?

3. How many square tiles will it take to cover the whole living room?

58 SG • Grade 3 • Unit 5 • Lesson 1   Measuring Area

Student Guide - page 58 (Answers on p. 29)

Teaching the Activity

Begin this activity by having students describe their understanding of area and how it can be measured. One way to reinforce students' concept of area is to draw a nonrectangular shape made of a whole number of square centimeters on a transparency of *Centimeter Grid Paper* and then ask students to find the area by counting square centimeters.

Another way to review area is to ask students how they could measure the area of the floor in the classroom. If you have a tile floor, they can measure its area by counting the number of tiles. In this case, the unit of measure would be the tiles, which are probably square. As your students work on this problem, they may discover that some tiles are not complete, but are tile pieces. Discuss how to count the tiles that are not whole. One convenient method is to find mates that add up to a whole when put together.

It is possible, but not practical, to cover the floor with square-inch tiles so it can be measured in square inches. Discuss how the number of tiles you need changes if the size of the tile changes. Stress that even if the unit of measure changes, the **area**— the amount of surface to be covered—stays the same.

Have students read the introduction to area on the *Measuring Area* Activity Pages. Direct their attention to the picture that shows Professor Peabody working on his floor and the diagram of his living room and hall. To answer *Question 1,* students can count the square tiles to find the area of the hallway. For *Question 2,* students should see that Professor Peabody counted halves of tiles by "piecing" them together to make whole squares; thus, two squares can each be numbered with the same number to show that two halves together are one whole. Figure 1 shows how to count area this way.

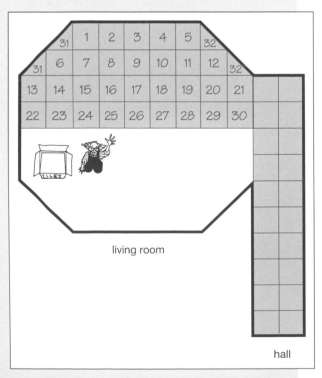

Figure 1: *Counting the area of a polygon*

In *Question 3,* students must help the professor calculate how many tiles he will need to cover the entire living room floor, the octagonal portion of the diagram. As Figure 1 shows, the area of the tiled portion of the living room floor is 32 tiles. Since the tiled and untiled portions are symmetrical, Professor Peabody will need an additional 32 tiles to finish the room.

Question 4 provides practice in finding the area of polygons in square centimeters. You can work along with the class by drawing the figures on a transparency of *Centimeter Grid Paper* and numbering the square centimeters. Help students piece together the half squares in Shape B.

Professor Peabody shows how he estimated the area of a shape with curved sides in *Question 5.* The procedure for finding the area of this shape is similar to that used in counting the area of polygons. However, it will not be as easy to find appropriate matches to piece together into wholes. Emphasize that students will only be able to **estimate** the area of the curved shapes.

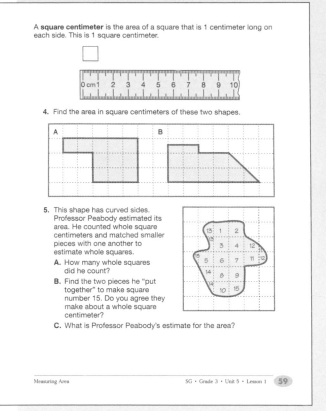

Student Guide - page 59 *(Answers on p. 29)*

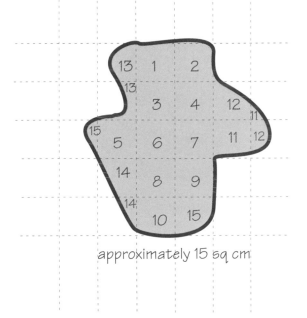

approximately 15 sq cm

Figure 2: *Counting the area of a curved shape*

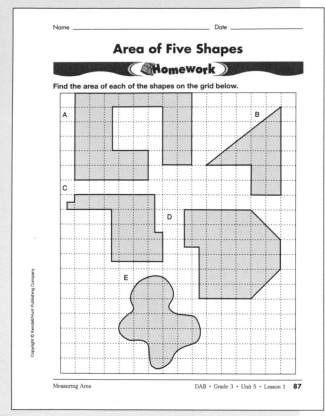

Name _____ Date _____

Area of Five Shapes

Homework

Find the area of each of the shapes on the grid below.

Measuring Area   DAB • Grade 3 • Unit 5 • Lesson 1   **87**

Discovery Assignment Book - page 87 *(Answers on p. 30)*

Math Facts

DPP Bit A provides practice with the subtraction facts in Group 7.

Homework and Practice

- For DPP Challenge B, students use multiplication to solve word problems.

- Assign the *Area of Five Shapes* Homework Page in the *Discovery Assignment Book,* which provides additional practice in measuring the area of polygons and curved shapes. Encourage students to write numbers in the square-centimeter grid boxes as they count. In reviewing Shape E with the class, compare students' methods and answers. There will be a variety of methods, but the answers should all be within one or two square centimeters of each other.

At a Glance

Math Facts and Daily Practice and Problems

For DPP Bit A, students practice the subtraction facts in Group 7. For DPP Challenge B, students solve multiplication word problems.

Teaching the Activity

1. Students describe their understanding of area and how it can be measured.
2. Draw a shape made of a whole number of square centimeters on a transparency of *Centimeter Grid Paper.* Ask students to find the area by counting square centimeters. (optional)
3. Discuss how students could measure the floor area in the classroom. (optional)
4. Students complete the *Measuring Area* Activity Pages.

Homework

Assign the *Area of Five Shapes* Homework Page.

Answer Key is on pages 29–30.

Notes:

Name _____ Date _____

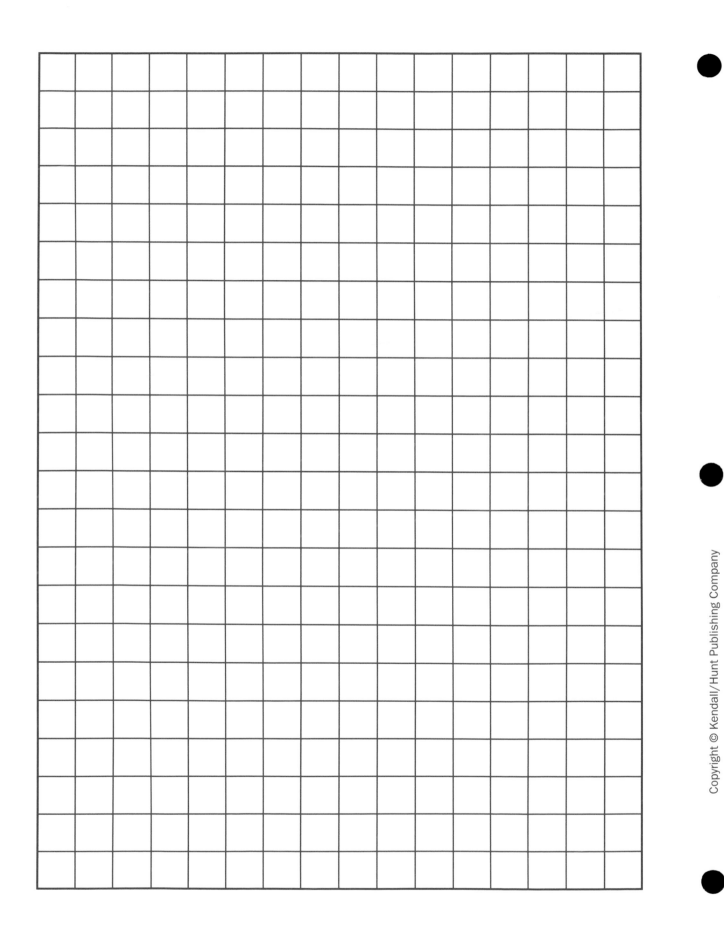

Centimeter Grid Paper, Blackline Master

Student Guide (p. 58)

Measuring Area*

1. 20 square tiles

2. Prof. Peabody numbered two tiles with the same number to show that two halves together cover one whole.

3. 64 square tiles

Measuring Area

What is area?

Area is a measurement of size. We measure the area of a floor to find the amount of carpet needed to cover the floor. We can also use area to measure the amount of paper needed to wrap a present.

Area is the amount of surface that is needed to cover something. To measure the area of a shape, we tell the number of squares needed to cover the shape.

Professor Peabody has started to cover his living room and hall with square tiles. The living room is in the shape of an octagon. The hall is a rectangle.

living room

hall

1. How many square tiles did Professor Peabody use to cover the hall?

2. Professor Peabody has covered half of his living room with tiles. These tiles have been counted for you. Why are the numbers 31 and 32 used twice?

3. How many square tiles will it take to cover the whole living room?

58   SG • Grade 3 • Unit 5 • Lesson 1   Measuring Area

Student Guide - page 58

Student Guide (p. 59)

4. **A.** 11 sq cm

   B. about 11 sq cm

5. **A.** 10 whole square centimeters

   B. Yes

   C. 15 sq cm

A **square centimeter** is the area of a square that is 1 centimeter long on each side. This is 1 square centimeter.

4. Find the area in square centimeters of these two shapes.

5. This shape has curved sides. Professor Peabody estimated its area. He counted whole square centimeters and matched smaller pieces with one another to estimate whole squares.

   A. How many whole squares did he count?

   B. Find the two pieces he "put together" to make square number 15. Do you agree they make about a whole square centimeter?

   C. What is Professor Peabody's estimate for the area?

Measuring Area   SG • Grade 3 • Unit 5 • Lesson 1   59

Student Guide - page 59

*Answers and/or discussion are included in the Lesson Guide.

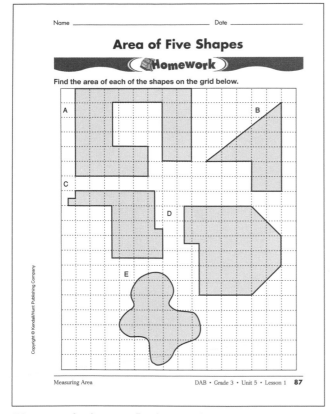

Discovery Assignment Book - page 87

Discovery Assignment Book (p. 87)

Area of Five Shapes*

A. $33\frac{1}{2}$ sq cm

B. about 14 sq cm

C. about 17 sq cm or $17\frac{1}{4}$ sq cm

D. about $31\frac{1}{2}$ sq cm

E. 17–19 sq cm

*Answers and/or discussion are included in the Lesson Guide.

Boo the Blob

Lesson Overview

Estimated Class Sessions

1

Students find the area of an irregular "blob" named Boo. Boo can change shape but not area. After Boo changes his shape, students find which of three different mystery shapes is Boo in another form. This activity provides a context for students to see that different shapes can have the same area, to practice estimating the area of irregular shapes, and to practice identifying the median value of a set of data.

Key Content

- Measuring area by counting whole and fractional parts of square centimeters.
- Finding the area of irregular shapes.
- Investigating the relationship between shape and area.
- Recognizing that different shapes can have the same area.
- Averaging: finding the median.

Key Vocabulary

- average
- mean
- median

Math Facts

DPP Bit C introduces the *Subtraction Flash Cards: Group 7*.

Homework

1. Students use their flash cards at home to study the subtraction facts in Group 7.
2. Assign Home Practice Parts 1 and 2.

Assessment

Observe students finding the area of irregular shapes and comparing different shapes with the same area while completing the *Boo the Blob Changes Shape* Activity Pages. Record observations on the *Observational Assessment Record*.

Curriculum Sequence

Before This Unit

Using Medians

In Grade 2 Unit 5 Lesson 4 *Rolling Along with Centimeters,* students found the median of three numbers to average the data for three trials in a laboratory investigation.

After This Unit

Using Averages

In Grade 3 Unit 16 Lesson 2 *Fill 'er Up!,* students will use medians in a laboratory investigation about volume. In Grade 4 students will use medians and means to average the data from multiple trials in labs. See Grade 4 Units 1 and 5.

Materials List

Supplies and Copies

Student	Teacher
Supplies for Each Student • scissors • 1 envelope for storing flash cards	**Supplies**
Copies • 1 copy of *Centimeter Grid Paper* per student (*Unit Resource Guide* Page 28)	**Copies/Transparencies** • 1 copy of *Observational Assessment Record* to be used throughout this unit (*Unit Resource Guide* Pages 9–10)

All blackline masters including assessment, transparency, and DPP masters are also on the Teacher Resource CD.

Student Books

Subtraction Flash Cards: Group 7 (*Discovery Assignment Book* Pages 83–84)
Boo the Blob Changes Shape (*Discovery Assignment Book* Pages 89–91)

Daily Practice and Problems and Home Practice

DPP items C–D (*Unit Resource Guide* Pages 13–14)
Home Practice Parts 1–2 (*Discovery Assignment Book* Page 80)

Note: Classrooms whose pacing differs significantly from the suggested pacing of the units should use the Math Facts Calendar in Section 4 of the *Facts Resource Guide* to ensure students receive the complete math facts program.

Assessment Tools

Observational Assessment Record (*Unit Resource Guide* Pages 9–10)

Daily Practice and Problems

Suggestions for using the DPPs are on page 36.

C. Bit: Subtraction Flash Cards: Group 7 (URG p. 13) $\frac{5}{\times 7}$

1. With a partner, sort the flash cards into three stacks: Facts I Know Quickly, Facts I Know Using a Strategy, and Facts I Need to Learn.

2. Update your *Subtraction Facts I Know* chart. Circle the facts you answered quickly. Underline those you knew by using a strategy. Do nothing to those you still need to learn.

D. Task: Comics (URG p. 14)

On an average day in the United States, 890 copies of a certain comic book series are sold. The number 890 is . . .

A. 10 more than __

B. 10 less than __

C. 100 more than __

D. 100 less than __

E. about half of __

F. about twice __

G. 800 + __

H. 10 × __

I. 500 + __

J. 110 less than __

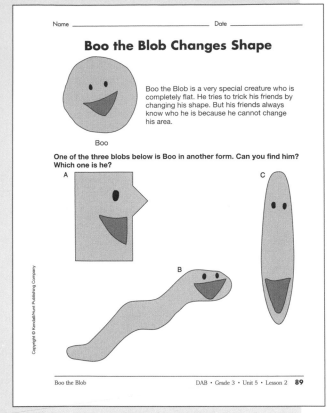

Name _____ **Date** _____

Boo the Blob Changes Shape

Boo the Blob is a very special creature who is completely flat. He tries to trick his friends by changing his shape. But his friends always know who he is because he cannot change his area.

Boo

One of the three blobs below is Boo in another form. Can you find him? Which one is he?

A

B

C

Boo the Blob   DAB • Grade 3 • Unit 5 • Lesson 2   **89**

Discovery Assignment Book - page 89

Teaching the Activity

Challenge students to find the area of Boo the Blob on the *Boo the Blob Changes Shape* Activity Pages in the *Discovery Assignment Book.* Allow them to use any method but emphasize the need for accuracy. One good method is for students to use scissors to cut out the blob. Then, using *Centimeter Grid Paper,* they can trace the blob and count square centimeters as they did in the previous lesson. They should find the area for the entire blob, including its mouth and eyes.

Compare students' results for the area of the shape labeled "Boo." List all the answers on the board from smallest to largest. Record each student's measurement, including duplicates. They should cluster around 20 square centimeters—the approximate area of the shape. Most answers will probably fall between 19 and 21 square centimeters. Since this method for finding the area of curved shapes does not give exact answers, expect some measurement error in the results. Let students give reasons for the different numbers. Here are some sample questions to guide discussion:

- *Is there only one right answer?*
- *How can you decide which answers are reasonable and which are not?*
- *Why is it a good idea to check your answer against those of other students?*
- *When should you try to recheck your answers?*

Explain that we should expect results to differ a little bit. Scientists address this by conducting multiple trials when they do an experiment. They then determine representative—or **average**—values for the data. Since there are different measurements for the shape, the class needs to decide on a good representative value. Have students share their ideas on how to agree on one representative measurement for Boo the Blob.

Tell students that the middle measurement is a good representative value. Remind them that the class's measurements on the board are in order from smallest to largest. Then demonstrate how to find the **median** or the middle measurement. First cross out the highest and the lowest measurements. Then cross out the second highest and second lowest measurements. Continue to cross out one measurement from each end of the data until you are left with one value—the middle value. If the list has an even

number of measurements, two will be in the middle of the data. The median is the value halfway between the two numbers. For example, if the two values are 19 square centimeters and 20 square centimeters, the median is $19\frac{1}{2}$ square centimeters.

Once students have agreed on Boo's approximate area, the class can form groups of three to measure the mystery blobs in search of the disguised Boo. Encourage students to cut out the shapes carefully and to count square centimeters as accurately as possible so they will be able to identify Boo correctly.

Have each student record his or her own measurements for the area of Shapes A, B, and C in the data table on the *Boo the Blob Changes Shape* Activity Pages. Group members should share their data and record it on their data tables. It is a good idea for the students to compare their answers so they can check for accuracy.

Before completing the data tables, ask groups to discuss the following:

* *Did all three members of your group get the same area for each shape? Why or why not?*

* *How might your group agree on one measurement for the area of each shape?* (Find the median value.)

Ask one group to share their data for Shape A. List the three measurements from smallest to largest on the board. Ask students to determine the median or middle measurement. This may be done by tossing out the high and low measurements. Instruct the remaining student groups to use their group data to find the median value for Shape A. Ask students to complete *Questions 1–4* on the *Boo the Blob Changes Shape* Activity Pages. Discuss the class results. Blob A has an area of 25 square centimeters; Blob C has an area of approximately 17 square centimeters; Blob B, which has an area of approximately 20 square centimeters, is Boo.

Check to see that students have not confused the median with the second measurement. Sometimes the median might have occurred in the second trial; however, this will not always be the case. If students have difficulty identifying the median, randomly list measurements in groups of three on the board. Use a number line to help them identify the median for each group of three.

Name _____ Date _____

Record the area you counted for Shapes A, B, and C in the data table. Record and compare two classmates' data as well. Do not write anything in the column labeled "Median" yet.

| Shape | Area in sq cm | | | |
	My Data	Classmate #1	Classmate #2	Median
A				
B				
C				

1. List the three areas your group found for Shape A in order from smallest to largest. Circle the middle value.

_____

2. The middle value is the **median.** Record the median area for Shape A in the data table.

3. Record the median values for Shapes B and C in the data table.

4. Which shape is Boo? Explain how your group decided.

_____
_____
_____
_____

Boo the Blob   DAB • Grade 3 • Unit 5 • Lesson 2   **91**

Discovery Assignment Book - page 91 *(Answers on p. 38)*

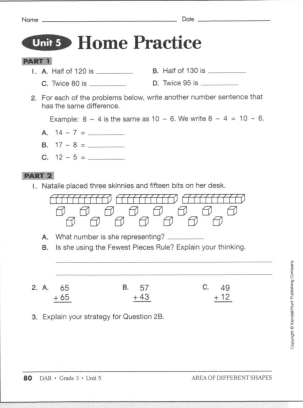

Discovery Assignment Book - page 80 (Answers on p. 38)

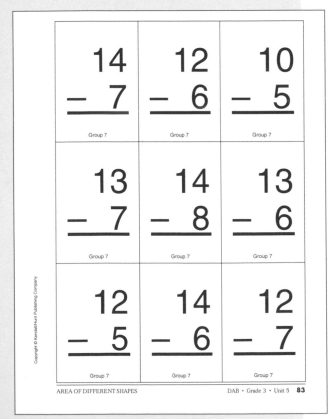

Discovery Assignment Book - page 83

Math Facts

DPP Bit C introduces the *Subtraction Flash Cards* for Group 7.

Homework and Practice

- In DPP Task D students develop number sense.

- Students take home *Subtraction Flash Cards: Group 7* and the list of facts they need to study and practice with a family member.

- Home Practice Parts 1 and 2 provide practice with place value, facts, and computation skills.

Answers for Parts 1 and 2 of the Home Practice are in the Answer Key at the end of this lesson and at the end of this unit.

Assessment

The *Boo the Blob* activity provides opportunities to observe students finding the area of irregular shapes by counting square centimeters. Students also compare different shapes that have the same area.

Extension

- By drawing a shape with an area of approximately 20 square centimeters, students can show how they think Boo might look after his next transformation. Then they can trade their new shape with a partner who can check to be sure that the area is approximately 20 square centimeters.

- Each student can create his or her own mystery blob of unknown area and then work with a partner to find its area.

Math Facts and Daily Practice and Problems

DPP Bit C introduces the *Subtraction Flash Cards: Group 7.* DPP Task D is a set of number sense problems.

Teaching the Activity

1. Using the *Boo the Blob Changes Shape* Activity Pages in the *Discovery Assignment Book,* students find Boo's area.
2. List all students' results for the area of the shape labeled "Boo" on the board from smallest to largest, including duplicates.
3. Discuss reasons for the differences in the numbers and how to agree on a representative value.
4. Demonstrate how to find the median of the measurements of Boo's area.
5. Each student finds and records the areas of Shapes A, B, and C.
6. Students share their data with two classmates and record their classmates' data on their data table.
7. Student groups discuss the differences in their estimated areas and the need for a representative value.
8. Students complete *Questions 1–4.*

Homework

1. Students study the subtraction facts in Group 7 at home using their flash cards.
2. Assign Home Practice Parts 1 and 2.

Assessment

Observe students finding the area of irregular shapes and comparing different shapes with the same area while completing the *Boo the Blob Changes Shape* Activity Pages. Record observations on the *Observational Assessment Record.*

Extension

1. Have students draw a shape with an area approximately 20 square centimeters to show how they think Boo might look after his next transformation.
2. Have each student create his or her own mystery blob of unknown area and then work with a partner to find its area.

Answer Key is on page 38.

Notes:

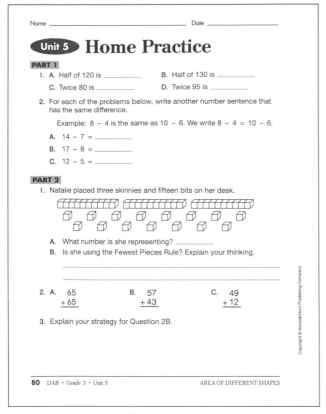

Name _____ Date _____

Unit 5 Home Practice

PART 1

1. A. Half of 120 is _____   B. Half of 130 is _____
   C. Twice 80 is _____   D. Twice 95 is _____

2. For each of the problems below, write another number sentence that
   has the same difference.

   Example: 8 − 4 is the same as 10 − 6. We write 8 − 4 = 10 − 6.

   A. 14 − 7 = _____
   B. 17 − 8 = _____
   C. 12 − 5 = _____

PART 2

1. Natalie placed three skinnies and fifteen bits on her desk.

   A. What number is she representing? _____
   B. Is she using the Fewest Pieces Rule? Explain your thinking.

   _____
   _____

2. A. 65   B. 57   C. 49
      +65   +43   +12

3. Explain your strategy for Question 2B.

80   DAB • Grade 3 • Unit 5   AREA OF DIFFERENT SHAPES

Discovery Assignment Book - page 80

Discovery Assignment Book (p. 80)

Home Practice*

Part 1

1. **A.** 60   **B.** 65
   C. 160   **D.** 190

2. Answers will vary.
   A. 15 − 8
   B. 19 − 10
   C. 10 − 3

Part 2

1. **A.** 45
   B. No. She could trade 10 bits for 1 skinny.
      She would then have 4 skinnies and 5 bits.

2. **A.** 130
   B. 100
   C. 61

3. Strategies will vary. Possible response:
   50 + 40 + 10 = 100

Name _____ Date _____

Record the area you counted for Shapes A, B, and C in the data table.
Record and compare two classmates' data as well. Do not write
anything in the column labeled "Median" yet.

Shape	Area in sq cm			
	My Data	Classmate #1	Classmate #2	Median
A				
B				
C				

1. List the three areas your group found for Shape A in order from
   smallest to largest. Circle the middle value.

2. The middle value is the **median.** Record the median area for Shape A
   in the data table.

3. Record the median values for Shapes B and C in the data table.

4. Which shape is Boo? Explain how your group decided.

   _____
   _____
   _____

Boo the Blob   DAB • Grade 3 • Unit 5 • Lesson 2   **91**

Discovery Assignment Book - page 91

Discovery Assignment Book (p. 91)

Boo the Blob Changes Shape†

1.–2. Answers will vary. Shape A is about
      25 sq cm.

3. Answers will vary. Shape B is about 20 sq cm.
   Shape C is about 17 sq cm.

4. Shape B is Boo. The median value for Boo
   and Shape B is 20 sq cm.

---

*Answers for all the Home Practice in the *Discovery Assignment Book* are at the end of the unit.
†Answers and/or discussion are included in the Lesson Guide.

Lesson 3

The Better "Picker Upper"

Lesson Overview

Estimated Class Sessions
4-5

Students investigate the area of a spot made by a given number of drops of water on different brands of paper towels. They measure the area of the spots by counting square centimeters. They use this information to decide which brand is most absorbent.

Key Content

- Identifying the variables of an investigation.
- Identifying variables that must be fixed to ensure fairness in an investigation.
- Collecting, organizing, graphing, and analyzing data.
- Finding the area of irregular shapes.
- Using data to solve problems.

Key Vocabulary

- area
- median
- variable

Math Facts

DPP Tasks H and J are multiplication problems. DPP Bits I and K provide practice with the subtraction facts in Group 8.

Homework

1. Students study the subtraction facts in Group 8 at home using their flash cards.
2. Assign *Lori's Questions* Homework Pages.

Assessment

1. The lab provides opportunities to observe the many aspects of conducting a lab. Use the *Observational Assessment Record* to record students' abilities to measure area and organize data.
2. Use **Questions 3** and **4** of the *Lori's Questions* Homework Pages to evaluate students' abilities to find the area of irregular shapes.

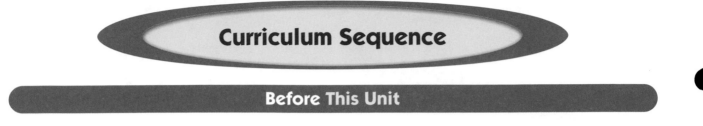

Curriculum Sequence

Identifying Variables

In Grade 3 Unit 1 Lessons 1 and 3, students identified variables in surveys and laboratory investigations.

Identifying Variables

Students will continue to identify variables in investigations in Grade 3. For examples, see Unit 9 Lesson 2 *Mass vs. Number,* Unit 10 Lesson 1 *Stencilrama,* and Unit 16 Lesson 2 *Fill 'er Up!*

Materials List

Supplies and Copies

Student	Teacher
Supplies for Each Student • 1 envelope for storing flash cards **Supplies for Each Student Group** • eyedropper • 3–4 brands of paper towels of varying quality, one sheet of each brand • scissors • small container of water • 2 books or 1 geoboard for drying paper towels	**Supplies** • food coloring, optional
Copies • 1 copy of *Centimeter Grid Paper* per student (*Unit Resource Guide* Page 28) • 1 copy of *Centimeter Graph Paper* per student (*Unit Resource Guide* Page 53)	**Copies/Transparencies** • 1 transparency of *Centimeter Graph Paper* (*Unit Resource Guide* Page 53)

All blackline masters including assessment, transparency, and DPP masters are also on the Teacher Resource CD.

Student Books
The Better "Picker Upper" (*Student Guide* Pages 60–61)
Subtraction Flash Cards: Group 8 (*Discovery Assignment Book* Pages 85–86)
The Better "Picker Upper" (*Discovery Assignment Book* Pages 93–96)
Lori's Questions (*Discovery Assignment Book* Pages 97–98)

Daily Practice and Problems and Home Practice
DPP items E–L (*Unit Resource Guide* Pages 14–18)
Home Practice Part 3 (*Discovery Assignment Book* Page 81)

Note: Classrooms whose pacing differs significantly from the suggested pacing of the units should use the Math Facts Calendar in Section 4 of the *Facts Resource Guide* to ensure students receive the complete math facts program.

Assessment Tools
Observational Assessment Record (*Unit Resource Guide* Pages 9–10)

Daily Practice and Problems

Suggestions for using the DPPs are on page 49.

E. Bit: Averaging Data (URG p. 14)

Julie did a study of candy color. Here is her data. Find the median number of candies for each color. The first one is done for you.

C Color	N Number			
	Sample 1	Sample 2	Sample 3	Median
red	3	5	4	4
brown	11	10	13	
orange	5	1	4	
green	5	6	5	

F. Task: More Comics (URG p. 15) [N]

On an average day in the United States, 1096 copies of a certain comic book series are sold.

Show this number with base-ten pieces.

Show this number with base-ten shorthand.

G. Bit: Averaging (URG p. 15)

In an experiment, Franco measured the area of different types of leaves. Here is his data. Find the median area for each type of leaf.

T Type of Leaf	A Area in sq cm			
	Trial 1	Trial 2	Trial 3	Median
Oak	48 sq cm	55 sq cm	50 sq cm	
Maple	86 sq cm	80 sq cm	84 sq cm	
Birch	10 sq cm	10 sq cm	12 sq cm	

H. Task: Kim's Savings (URG p. 16) [×5/7] [$]

1. Kim earns $7 each week mowing lawns. She wants to buy jeans that cost $45. The tax will be $3. How long will she have to save to buy the jeans?
   Will she have to save longer than a month?
2. Leila earns $10 each week babysitting. How much money will she earn in 10 weeks?

I. Bit: Subtraction: Using Doubles [×5/7]
   (URG p. 16)

Do these problems in your head. Write only the answers.

1. $16 - 8 =$ 2. $17 - 8 =$
3. $15 - 8 =$ 4. $18 - 9 =$
5. $18 - 10 =$ 6. $15 - 7 =$
7. $8 - 4 =$ 8. $7 - 4 =$
9. $60 - 30 =$

10. Explain your strategy for solving Question 4.

J. Task: Story Solving (URG p. 17) [×5/7]

$8 \times 8 = ?$ Write a story and draw a picture about 8×8.

Write a number sentence on your picture.

K. Bit: Subtraction Flash Cards: [×5/7]
   Group 8 (URG p. 17)

1. With a partner, sort the flash cards into three stacks: Facts I Know Quickly, Facts I Know Using a Strategy, and Facts I Need to Learn.
2. Update your *Subtraction Facts I Know* chart. Circle the facts you answered quickly. Underline those you knew by using a strategy. Do nothing to those you still need to learn.

L. Challenge: Magic Square: [✕]
   Sum = 27 (URG p. 18)

Complete the magic square using the numbers 5, 6, 7, 8, 9, 10, 11, 12, and 13. Each row, column, and diagonal must have a sum of 27.

Before the Lab

You need three brands of paper towels. Try to include an inexpensive or generic brand, an expensive "super-absorbent" brand, and a recycled paper so that students can explore advertising claims and environmental concerns as well as absorbency.

Some teachers prefer to make the spots with colored water. To create the colored water, combine 3 to 4 drops of food coloring with about 100 cc of water. Distribute this water into separate containers for groups to use. Each group will need a small amount—probably 10–20 cc.

Teaching the Lab

Part 1 Preliminary Discussion of the Lab

Students will investigate the absorbency of several brands of paper towels by measuring the area of the spots formed by drops of water. This experiment works well with cooperative groups of two to four members and takes approximately four to five class sessions.

To begin a preliminary discussion, read and discuss the questions on *The Better "Picker Upper"* Lab Pages in the *Student Guide.* Professor Peabody decides to investigate different brands of paper towels after he cleans up a spill in his lab with one that is not very absorbent. Students will conduct an experiment similar to Professor Peabody's.

As you discuss the questions in the *Student Guide,* consider the following: In this experiment, we want to find which paper towel is the better "picker upper," that is, the most absorbent. The discussion of *Question 1* should lead to the conclusion that we are interested in which paper towel can soak up the most water. Include in your discussion other questions such as:

- *How can we decide which paper towel soaks up the most water?*

- *Is there anything that we can measure?*

To answer *Question 2,* let student groups make a preliminary investigation by touching and looking at a sheet from each paper towel roll. The sheets may differ in size and thickness.

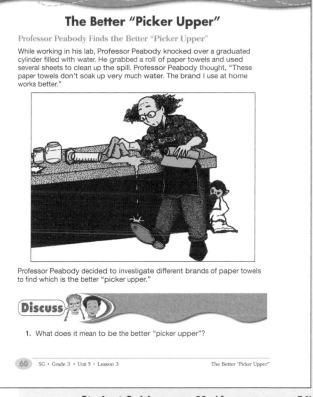

The Better "Picker Upper"

Professor Peabody Finds the Better "Picker Upper"

While working in his lab, Professor Peabody knocked over a graduated cylinder filled with water. He grabbed a roll of paper towels and used several sheets to clean up the spill. Professor Peabody thought, "These paper towels don't soak up very much water. The brand I use at home works better."

Professor Peabody decided to investigate different brands of paper towels to find which is the better "picker upper."

Discuss

1. What does it mean to be the better "picker upper"?

Student Guide - page 60 (Answers on p. 54)

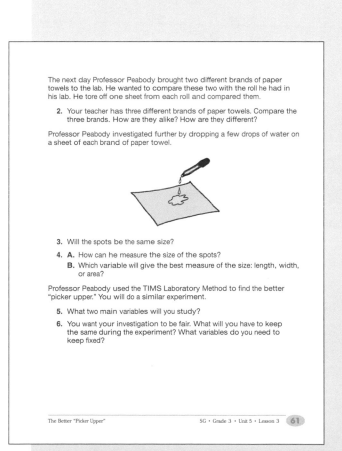

The next day Professor Peabody brought two different brands of paper towels to the lab. He wanted to compare these two with the roll he had in his lab. He tore off one sheet from each roll and compared them.

2. Your teacher has three different brands of paper towels. Compare the three brands. How are they alike? How are they different?

Professor Peabody investigated further by dropping a few drops of water on a sheet of each brand of paper towel.

3. Will the spots be the same size?

4. A. How can he measure the size of the spots?
   B. Which variable will give the best measure of the size: length, width, or area?

Professor Peabody used the TIMS Laboratory Method to find the better "picker upper." You will do a similar experiment.

5. What two main variables will you study?

6. You want your investigation to be fair. What will you have to keep the same during the experiment? What variables do you need to keep fixed?

Student Guide - page 61 (Answers on p. 54)

To answer **Questions 3** and **4,** students may conduct another preliminary investigation using water, eyedroppers, and paper towels, or you can ask volunteers to show what happens when a few drops of water are dropped on a paper towel. They should see that the spots vary in size from sheet to sheet. Once students identify area as the variable that will give the best measure of size, ask:

*   *How can we measure the area of the spots?* (Have students share their ideas. Students may suggest cutting out the spots, tracing them on *Centimeter Grid Paper,* and counting square centimeters.)
*   *Will knowing the area of the spots on the different paper towels help determine which brand soaks up the most water?*

Once measuring the area of the spots on each paper towel is suggested, we hope the class will agree that this is a good way to compare paper towels. However, additional prompting or questions from you may be needed to guide students in this direction. Then you can frame the experiment in terms of the two primary variables: Type of Paper Towels *(T)* and Area of the Spot *(A),* the focus of **Question 5.**

In addition to the primary variables, however, others will affect the outcome. Let students use eyedroppers to drop water on the paper towels with **Question 6** in mind. After working with the materials, students should be able to come up with a list of procedures that will make the experiment fair. Be sure they include the following:

1. Use the same type of liquid (water) on all the paper towels.
2. Use the same number of drops to make each spot. It is important for students to realize that all groups must use the same number of drops to be able to compare their results. Therefore, they should be encouraged to decide as a class how many drops should be used on each towel. Two or three drops usually work well.
3. Drop all the drops in the center of each spot.
4. Use the same eyedropper to keep the size of the drops the same.
5. Keep the towels off the desk until the spot has stopped spreading so the water will spread out on the paper towel and not on the desk. (See Figure 4.)

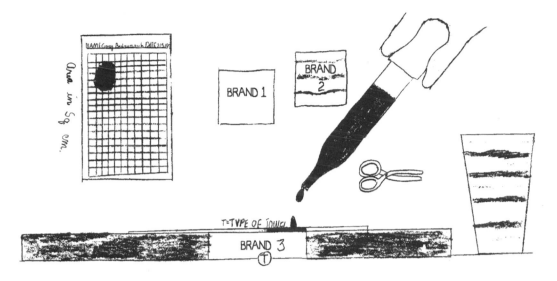

Figure 3: *Daniel's picture identifies procedures and variables.*

Part 2 Drawing the Picture

After the discussion, you can model the procedure for collecting the data as described below in Part 3 Collecting and Recording the Data. Then students are ready to draw a picture of the experimental setup and its variables on *The Better "Picker Upper"* Lab Pages in the *Discovery Assignment Book.* In the sample picture in Figure 3, Daniel shows the procedure and clearly labels the three types of paper towels. By looking at the picture, we know the experimenter will drop water onto a paper towel, use scissors to cut out the resulting spot, measure the area by placing the spot on grid paper, and count the square centimeters of area. Daniel clearly labels the two primary variables: "T = Type of Towel" and "Area in sq cm." Students should answer *Questions 1–4* on *The Better "Picker Upper"* Lab Pages.

Part 3 Collecting and Recording the Data

Discuss with the class the need to measure more than one spot for each brand of paper towel. Making several trials in an experiment is an idea they will encounter many times in this curriculum. The data table provides room to record the results of three trials and their median value. (For a discussion of finding the median, see Lesson Guide 2 *Boo the Blob.*)

Name _____ Date _____

The Better "Picker Upper"

Draw

Draw a picture of what you are going to do in the experiment. Label the variables in your picture.

1. What variables will you study in this experiment?

_____

_____

2. What variables should not change in this experiment? Explain.

_____

_____

The Better "Picker Upper"   DAB • Grade 3 • Unit 5 • Lesson 3   **93**

Discovery Assignment Book **- page 93 (Answers on p. 55)**

TIMS Tip

If students write the brand name on each sheet as they receive it, they will have fewer problems remembering brands later. It is also a good idea for student groups to write their initials on the paper towels.

TIMS Tip

Another way of doing this experiment is for each group to cover the spots with a transparency of *Centimeter Grid Paper* and to trace the outline of the spot on the transparency. This method eliminates the cutting.

Name _____ Date _____

3. What are you trying to find out in this experiment?

_____
_____
_____

4. Look carefully at each of your paper towels. Which towel do you think is the better "picker upper"? Explain.

_____
_____
_____

Collect

Work with your partners to do the experiment. Record your data in the table below. Don't forget to write the proper units for your measurements. How many drops of water will you use on each towel?

T Type of Towel	A Area of Spot (in _____ unit)			
	Trial 1	Trial 2	Trial 3	Median

Copyright © Kendall/Hunt Publishing Company

94 DAB • Grade 3 • Unit 5 • Lesson 3   The Better "Picker Upper"

Discovery Assignment Book - page 94 (Answers on p. 56)

Each group should have one sheet of each different brand of paper towels. Students should place the three spots far enough apart on each sheet so they will not run together. To facilitate this process, students can keep their paper towels off the tabletop by laying them on top of geoboards. Another method is to place two books on the table, spaced a little closer than the width of one sheet. Then, one edge of a sheet is placed between the pages of each book so that it is lifted off the tabletop, as in Figure 4.

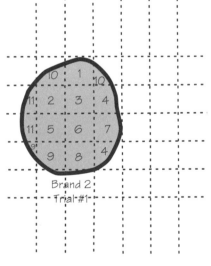

Figure 4: *Two ways to keep sheets off the tabletop*

As soon as the spots quit spreading, students should trace the perimeter of each spot with a pencil. This provides an outline of the spot's perimeter that will be visible once the water evaporates. Letting the towels dry for several minutes or overnight will make it easier for students to cut out their spots.

When the spots are dry enough, students should cut them out and trace them on a piece of *Centimeter Grid Paper*. Once the spots are traced, students should label them according to brand name. The groups are now ready to count square centimeters and record the area of each spot on their data tables. If students completed *Measuring Area* and *Boo the Blob* (Lessons 1 and 2), they should be familiar with the technique for finding area by counting square centimeters.

Figure 5: *Counting the area of a spot*

While students are gathering and recording data, check the results of each group. Although we expect a certain amount of error, the measured area of the three spots for each type of paper towel should be relatively close. In Daniel's data table shown in Figure 6, the results of the three trials for both Brand 1 and Brand 2 are as close to one another as we can expect.

However, the data for Brand 3 looks suspect: the area for the first trial is almost double the area found in the third trial. These differences provide an opportunity to discuss the possibility of making mistakes—perhaps Daniel did not trace or cut out one of the spots as carefully. This is also a good time to point out problems that can occur if the fixed variables are not actually held constant—perhaps the first spot contained too many drops. If possible, this group should perform a fourth trial and use this data to judge which trial contains the most error and replace it with the new trial.

T Type of Towel	*A* Area of Spot (in _sq cm_)			
	Trial 1	Trial 2	Trial 3	Median
Brand 1	3 sq cm	2 sq cm	3 sq cm	3 sq cm
Brand 2	11 sq cm	13 sq cm	13 sq cm	13 sq cm
Brand 3	11 sq cm	8 sq cm	6 sq cm	8 sq cm

Figure 6: *Daniel's data table*

Part 4 Graphing the Data

This experiment is a good opportunity for the class to begin using *Centimeter Graph Paper* for drawing bar graphs. Since they will no longer have guidelines to use, you may need to model how to draw bars on this type of graph paper. Be sure students draw their bars on the lines and place the labels indicating the towel brands below the lines not the spaces, as in Figure 7. We use this convention so the transition from bar graphing to point graphing in Unit 7 will be easier.

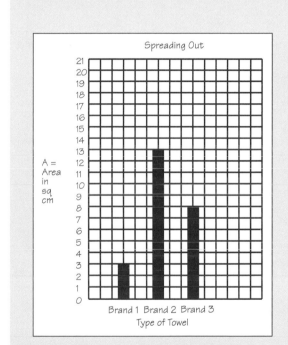

Figure 7: *A graph of Daniel's data*

Name ______________________ Date ____________

Graph

Graph your median data on a separate piece of graph paper.

Explore

Write your answers to the following questions.

5. Which towel had the spot with the largest area? What was the area of the spot?

6. Which towel had the spot with the smallest area?

7. How much larger was the larger spot than the smallest spot? Explain how you found your answer.

8. How would the graph look if you dropped twice as many drops on each towel?

***Discovery Assignment Book* - page 95** *(Answers on p. 56)*

Name ______________________ Date ____________

9. Choose one brand of paper towels. Predict how many drops of water it would take to cover one sheet *completely*. Explain how you made your prediction.

Brand of paper towel selected ____________

Predicted number of drops to cover entire towel ____________

10. Look at your data table and graph. Which towel do you think will soak up the most water? Why?

Discuss

Discuss this question with your class.

11. If you could design another experiment with paper towels, what would it be? What variables would you choose to study? What variables should not change? Describe your experiment on a separate sheet of paper.

***Discovery Assignment Book* - page 96** *(Answers on p. 57)*

Part 5 Exploring the Data

Questions 5–7 ask the students to read information directly from the graph. To answer ***Questions 8*** and ***9,*** on the other hand, most students will probably want to do some additional experimentation and may take an entire period to find their answers. It is a good idea for students to work on these questions in groups before discussing them with the class. Students often find many different ways to solve problems, and the groups may come up with several possibilities. Try to discuss the advantages and disadvantages of each method.

Let students experiment with the towels and eyedroppers as they develop their solutions. A typical student response to ***Question 9*** is given by Juanita below. Note that Juanita made use of the spots from her original investigation and multiplication.

Juanita's response: *I would take my middle test sample and on a new sheet I would trace as many circles as I could as close together as I could. Enough to fill the whole sheet. Then I would count how many circles I had and multiply that # by 3 drops to get my estimate.*

Question 10 continues with the ideas explored in ***Question 9.*** Two answers to this question are probable: (1) The towel with the tallest bar will soak up the most water, or (2) the towel with the shortest bar will soak up the most water. These opposing views can lead to a lively class discussion. Those students who defend the first position probably believe that "bigger is better." However, the discussion should result in the generalization that the towel with the shortest bar is the better "picker upper." On this towel, the three drops of water are concentrated in the smallest area, leaving more of the paper towel to soak up more water.

Journal Prompt

What is area?

Math Facts

DPP Task H presents two problems that use multiplication facts. Bit I reviews subtraction facts in Group 8. Task J asks students to write a story and draw a picture for a multiplication problem. Bit K introduces the *Subtraction Flash Cards* for Group 8.

Homework and Practice

- DPP Bits E and G ask students to analyze data and find medians. DPP Task F has students represent a number with base-ten pieces. Challenge L is a magic square.

- Students take home *Subtraction Flash Cards: Group 8* and the list of facts they need to study and practice with a family member.

- Assign the *Lori's Questions* Homework Pages in the *Discovery Assignment Book.* These pages give each student an opportunity to independently use the procedures and problem-solving skills he or she developed while working with a group.

Assessment

- Use DPP Bit G as an assessment of students' abilities to find the median of a set of data.

- As you review students' completed labs, assess their abilities to estimate the area of irregular shapes by checking their work on the grid paper. Does it clearly indicate how they counted the whole square centimeters and how they found fractional pieces that fit together to approximate whole square centimeters? Record this information on the *Observational Assessment Record.*

- You can also use *Questions 3* and *4* of the *Lori's Questions* Homework Pages to evaluate students' abilities to find the area of irregular shapes.

- Use Home Practice Part 3 as an assessment of measuring and comparing the area of irregular shapes.

- Use students' data tables and graphs to assess their progress in organizing and graphing data. Record your observations on the *Observational Assessment Record.* See the Assessment section of the *Teacher Implementation Guide* for suggestions for grading labs.

Answers for Part 3 of the Home Practice are in the Answer Key at the end of this lesson and at the end of this unit.

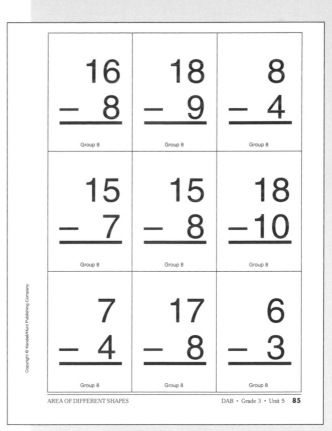

Discovery Assignment Book - page 85

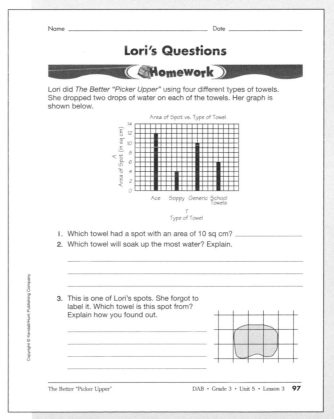

Discovery Assignment Book - page 97 (Answers on p. 57)

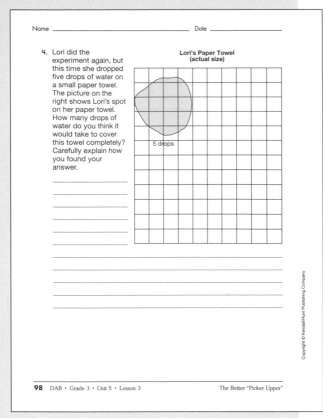

Discovery Assignment Book - page 98 (Answers on p. 58)

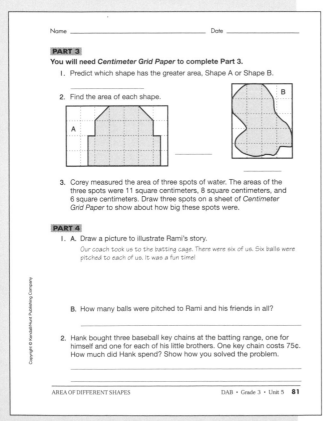

Discovery Assignment Book - page 81 (Answers on p. 55)

The discussion of *Question 11* of *The Better "Picker Upper"* lab will center around other possible experiments that the class could perform using the paper towels and the techniques they learned in this experiment. As an extension, students can design and carry out their own experiments. As students discuss the design of the new experiment, keep in mind that they will be looking for the relationship between two variables while holding other variables fixed. For example, instead of investigating the relationship between the type of paper towel and the area of the spot of water while keeping other variables fixed, students can explore the relationship between the type of liquid and the area of a spot while keeping other variables, including the type of paper towel, fixed. Students may be interested in finding the relationship between the type of paper towel and its strength. They can measure strength by counting how many masses can be placed on suspended wet paper towels before they break.

If students try a new experiment, you can assess their abilities to collect, organize, graph, and analyze data.

- *Are they able to communicate clearly which variables they chose to study?*
- *Did they use an appropriate data table?*
- *Did they clearly show their results on a graph?*
- *Were they able to make conclusions based on their data?*

Since this lesson comes early in the year, you will need to help students structure their experiments. We hope students will become more independent as the year progresses as they become more familiar with the TIMS Laboratory Method. If you assess their abilities now, you can document their growth throughout the year.

Estimated Class Sessions

4-5

At a Glance

Math Facts and Daily Practice and Problems

For Bits E and G students find the median of a data set. DPP Tasks H and J are multiplication problems. DPP Bits I and K work with the subtraction facts in Group 8. For DPP Task F students represent a number with base-ten pieces. Challenge L is a magic square.

Part 1. Preliminary Discussion of the Lab

1. Use *The Better "Picker Upper"* Lab Pages in the *Student Guide* to lead a discussion about the lab.
2. Students look at, feel, and compare three different brands of paper towels.
3. Students conduct a preliminary investigation using eyedroppers, water, and paper towels.
4. Discuss how to measure area.
5. Discuss the two main variables and those that should be held fixed to keep the experiment fair.

Part 2. Drawing the Picture

1. Model data collection for the class.
2. Students draw a picture and answer *Questions 1–4* on *The Better "Picker Upper"* Lab Pages in the *Discovery Assignment Book.*

Part 3. Collecting and Recording the Data

1. Discuss the necessity for measuring more than one spot for each brand of towel.
2. Each group makes three spots of water on each sheet.
3. Students trace the perimeters of the spots, cut them out, trace them on a piece of *Centimeter Grid Paper,* and label them.
4. Students find and record the area of each spot.
5. Students find and record the median value of the three spots on each sheet.

Part 4. Graphing the Data

1. Model bar graphing on centimeter graph paper using a transparency of *Centimeter Graph Paper.*
2. Students graph their median data on pieces of *Centimeter Graph Paper.*

Part 5. Exploring the Data

1. In groups, students answer *Questions 5–10* on *The Better "Picker Upper"* Lab Pages.
2. Students share their answers and solution strategies.
3. The class discusses *Questions 10* and *11.*

Homework

1. Students use their flash cards at home to study the subtraction facts in Group 8.
2. Assign *Lori's Questions* Homework Pages.

At a Glance

Assessment

1. The lab provides opportunities to observe the many aspects of conducting a lab. Use the *Observational Assessment Record* to record students' abilities to measure area and organize data.
2. Use *Questions 3* and *4* of the *Lori's Questions* Homework Pages to evaluate students' abilities to find the area of irregular shapes.

Extension

Have students design and carry out their own experiments. Keep in mind that students will be looking at the relationship between two variables while holding other variables fixed. Students may want to find the relationship between the type of paper towel and its strength.

Answer Key is on pages 54–58.

Notes:

Name _____   Date _____

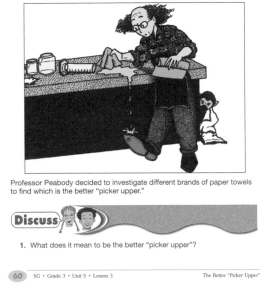

The Better "Picker Upper"

Professor Peabody Finds the Better "Picker Upper"

While working in his lab, Professor Peabody knocked over a graduated cylinder filled with water. He grabbed a roll of paper towels and used several sheets to clean up the spill. Professor Peabody thought, "These paper towels don't soak up very much water. The brand I use at home works better."

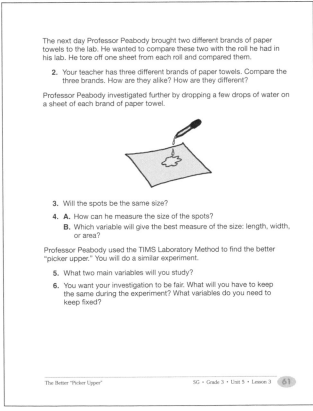

Professor Peabody decided to investigate different brands of paper towels to find which is the better "picker upper."

Discuss

1. What does it mean to be the better "picker upper"?

60   SG • Grade 3 • Unit 5 • Lesson 3   The Better "Picker Upper"

Student Guide - page 60

The next day Professor Peabody brought two different brands of paper towels to the lab. He wanted to compare these two with the roll he had in his lab. He tore off one sheet from each roll and compared them.

2. Your teacher has three different brands of paper towels. Compare the three brands. How are they alike? How are they different?

Professor Peabody investigated further by dropping a few drops of water on a sheet of each brand of paper towel.

3. Will the spots be the same size?
4. A. How can he measure the size of the spots?
   B. Which variable will give the best measure of the size: length, width, or area?

Professor Peabody used the TIMS Laboratory Method to find the better "picker upper." You will do a similar experiment.

5. What two main variables will you study?
6. You want your investigation to be fair. What will you have to keep the same during the experiment? What variables do you need to keep fixed?

The Better "Picker Upper"   SG • Grade 3 • Unit 5 • Lesson 3   61

Student Guide - page 61

Student Guide (p. 60)

The Better "Picker Upper"*

1. The brand of paper towel that soaks up the most water will be the better "picker upper."

Student Guide (p. 61)

2. Answers will vary. The sheets may differ in size and thickness.
3. Probably not.
4. A. Answers will vary. He could measure the length and/or width of the spot. He could cut the spot out, trace it on cm grid paper, and find the area by counting square centimeters.
   B. area
5. Type of Towel (T) and Area of Spot (A)
6. Answers will vary. See Lesson Guide 3 for a list of procedures that will make the experiment fair.

*Answers and/or discussion are included in the Lesson Guide.

Discovery Assignment Book (p. 81)

Home Practice*

Part 3

1. Answers will vary.

2. Shape A is about 17 sq cm. Shape B is about 13 sq cm.

3. Shapes will vary. Area of the spots should be 11 sq cm, 8 sq cm, and 6 sq cm. Accept a spot with square corners but discuss the likelihood that spreading water would form this type of shape. Compare students' "spots."

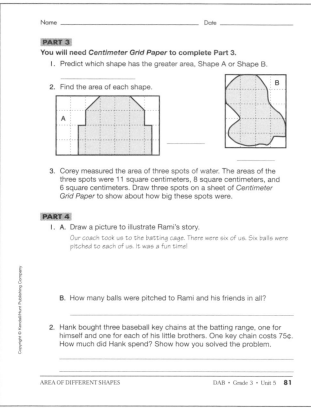

Discovery Assignment Book - page 81

Discovery Assignment Book (p. 93)

The Better "Picker Upper"†

See Lesson Guide 3 for a sample student picture and a completed data table and graph.

1. The two primary variables are Type of Towel and Area of Spot. The brands of paper towels are the values for the variable Type of Towel.

2. Among the fixed variables are the number of drops placed on each spot; the type of liquid used (water); the size of each drop (as controlled by the eyedropper); and certain elements of the procedure (e.g., keeping the paper towel off the table).

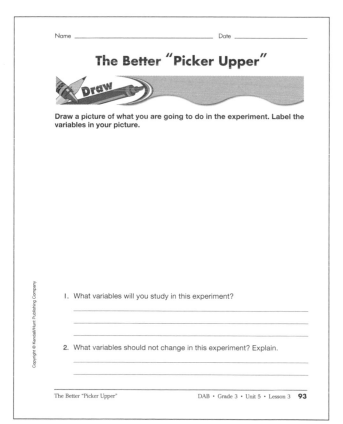

Discovery Assignment Book - page 93

*Answers for all the Home Practice in the *Discovery Assignment Book* are at the end of the unit.
†Answers and/or discussion are included in the Lesson Guide.

Name _____ Date _____

3. What are you trying to find out in this experiment?
_____
_____
_____

4. Look carefully at each of your paper towels. Which towel do you think is the better "picker upper"? Explain.
_____
_____
_____

Collect

Work with your partners to do the experiment. Record your data in the table below. Don't forget to write the proper units for your measurements. How many drops of water will you use on each towel?

T Type of Towel	A Area of Spot (in ____ unit)			
	Trial 1	Trial 2	Trial 3	Median

94   DAB • Grade 3 • Unit 5 • Lesson 3   The Better "Picker Upper"

Discovery Assignment Book - page 94

Name _____ Date _____

Graph

Graph your median data on a separate piece of graph paper.

Explore

Write your answers to the following questions.

5. Which towel had the spot with the largest area? What was the area of the spot?
_____

6. Which towel had the spot with the smallest area?
_____

7. How much larger was the larger spot than the smallest spot? Explain how you found your answer.
_____
_____
_____
_____

8. How would the graph look if you dropped twice as many drops on each towel?
_____
_____
_____
_____

The Better "Picker Upper"   DAB • Grade 3 • Unit 5 • Lesson 3   95

Discovery Assignment Book - page 95

Discovery Assignment Book (p. 94)

3. Answers will vary but will probably focus on which towel is "better" or soaks up more water.

4. Students will make predictions based on a wide variety of factors: thickness, texture, pattern of the weave, etc.

Discovery Assignment Book (p. 95)

Answers to *Questions 5–10* are based on the sample data and graph in Figures 6 and 7 in Lesson Guide 3.

5. Brand 2, 13 sq cm

6. Brand 1, 3 sq cm

7. 10 sq cm; some students may write a number sentence (e.g., $13 - 3 = 10$ sq cm). Others will explain with words or draw a picture.

8. Answers and explanations will vary. You might predict that the bars would get bigger. They would approximately double. For example, the bar for Brand 1 would go to 6 sq cm rather than 3 sq cm. Some students may want to do some additional experimentation. Encourage students to sketch a graph.

Discovery Assignment Book (p. 96)

9. Answers and strategies will vary. A typical student response is given in Lesson Guide 3.

10. This is an extension of the work students did in **Question 9.** Discussion should lead to the idea that the towel with the shortest bar is the better "picker upper." On this towel, the three drops of water are concentrated in the smallest area, leaving more of the paper towel to soak up more water.

11. Try to get students to think about the variables in the experiment. A new experiment could be designed by keeping the type of paper towel fixed and looking for the relationship between the type of liquid and the area of the spots or looking for the relationship between the height |of the dropper and the area of the spots. Another possibility is to look at different types of paper towels and measure their strength by placing masses on top of the different brands of wet towels until they tear.

Name _____ Date _____

9. Choose one brand of paper towels. Predict how many drops of water it would take to cover one sheet *completely*. Explain how you made your prediction.

Brand of paper towel selected _____

Predicted number of drops to cover entire towel _____

_____

_____

_____

_____

_____

_____

_____

10. Look at your data table and graph. Which towel do you think will soak up the most water? Why?

_____

_____

_____

_____

_____

_____

_____

_____

Discuss

Discuss this question with your class.

11. If you could design another experiment with paper towels, what would it be? What variables would you choose to study? What variables should not change? Describe your experiment on a separate sheet of paper.

96 DAB • Grade 3 • Unit 5 • Lesson 3   The Better "Picker Upper"

Discovery Assignment Book - page 96

Discovery Assignment Book (p. 97)

Lori's Questions

1. Generic

2. Soppy towels will absorb the most water. The spot spread over the smallest area so there is more "room" to soak up more drops than in the towels with the bigger spots. It will take fewer of the bigger spots to completely cover the towel so those towels will be able to soak up less water.

3. School towels—The area of the spot is about the same as the area of the school towels shown on the graph (approximately 6 sq cm).*

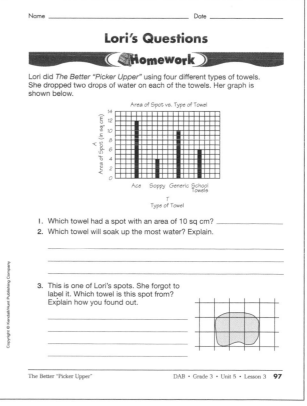

Name _____ Date _____

Lori's Questions

Homework

Lori did *The Better "Picker Upper"* using four different types of towels. She dropped two drops of water on each of the towels. Her graph is shown below.

1. Which towel had a spot with an area of 10 sq cm? _____
2. Which towel will soak up the most water? Explain.

_____

_____

3. This is one of Lori's spots. She forgot to label it. Which towel is this spot from? Explain how you found out.

_____

_____

_____

The Better "Picker Upper"   DAB • Grade 3 • Unit 5 • Lesson 3 **97**

Discovery Assignment Book - page 97

*Answers and/or discussion are included in the Lesson Guide.

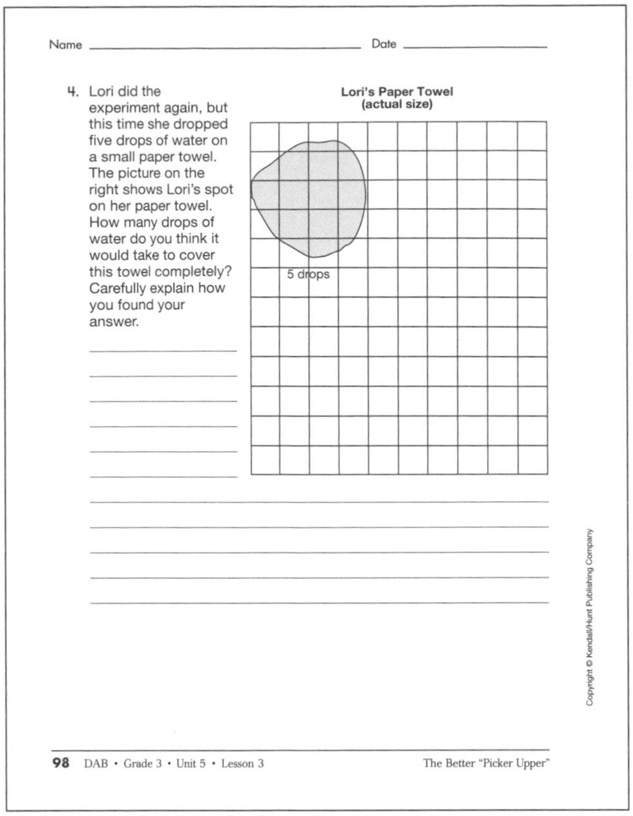

Name _____ Date _____

4. Lori did the experiment again, but this time she dropped five drops of water on a small paper towel. The picture on the right shows Lori's spot on her paper towel. How many drops of water do you think it would take to cover this towel completely? Carefully explain how you found your answer.

Lori's Paper Towel
(actual size)

5 drops

_____
_____
_____
_____

_____
_____
_____
_____
_____

Discovery Assignment Book - page 98

Discovery Assignment Book (p. 98)

4. The area of the spot is about 11, 12, or 13 sq cm. The area of the towel is 120 sq cm. About ten spots will cover the towel (120 ÷ 12). Since each spot contains 5 drops, it would take about 50 drops to cover the towel.*

Some students may solve the problem by "covering" the towel with replications of the spot. About 6–9 spots can be placed on the towel using this method. Depending on how the students compensate for uncovered spaces on the towel, answers between 33 and 50 drops are acceptable. Other reasonable strategies are possible.

*Answers and/or discussion are included in the Lesson Guide.

Lesson 4

The Haunted House

Lesson Overview

Estimated Class Sessions

1

Rosita and Peter solve a mystery about a haunted house by measuring a footprint left by a "ghost." They find the length and area of the ghost's footprint and compare these measurements to the length and area of their classmates' footprints. Since they use more than one type of measurement (length *and* area), they are able to reduce the chance of error and correctly identify the ghost as one of their classmates.

Key Content

- Connecting mathematics to a real-life situation: measuring the length and area of footprints to solve a mystery.

Homework

For Home Practice Part 4, students solve multiplication problems using square numbers.

Materials List

Supplies and Copies

Student	Teacher
Supplies for Each Student	**Supplies**
Copies	**Copies/Transparencies**

All blackline masters including assessment, transparency, and DPP masters are also on the Teacher Resource CD.

Student Books
The Haunted House (*Adventure Book* Pages 26–42)

Daily Practice and Problems and Home Practice
DPP items M–N (*Unit Resource Guide* Page 18)
Home Practice Part 4 (*Discovery Assignment Book* Page 81)

Note: Classrooms whose pacing differs significantly from the suggested pacing of the units should use the Math Facts Calendar in Section 4 of the *Facts Resource Guide* to ensure students receive the complete math facts program.

Daily Practice and Problems

Suggestions for using the DPPs are on page 65.

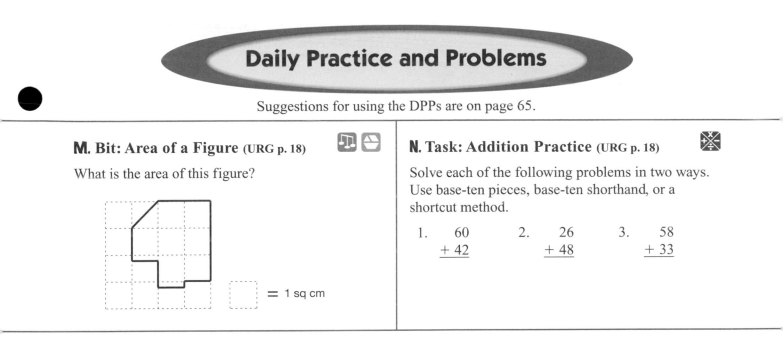

M. Bit: Area of a Figure (URG p. 18)

What is the area of this figure?

$\square$ = 1 sq cm

N. Task: Addition Practice (URG p. 18)

Solve each of the following problems in two ways. Use base-ten pieces, base-ten shorthand, or a shortcut method.

1.   60
    + 42

2.   26
    + 48

3.   58
    + 33

Adventure Book - page 31

Page 31

- *Who or what do you think made the footprint?*

Adventure Book - page 32

Page 32

- *Explain how you would find the area of the footprint.*

Students should be able to apply the method used to find area in *The Better "Picker Upper"* to this new situation. Peter and Rosita can trace the footprint and use graph paper to estimate its area.

- *What problems might they encounter in measuring length?*

They need to decide which part of the footprint to measure to find its length. Measuring from the heel to the tip of the big toe will provide a different answer than measuring from the heel to the tip of the little toe. Similar problems would result if they use width.

Page 34

- *Why does Rosita want to count the area independently from Peter?*

Both Rosita and Peter should count so that they know their estimate is accurate.

- *Why does Peter say the measurement is about 53 sq cm?*

His answer is an estimate of the area. Peter is rounding off his estimate to the nearest whole number.

- *Is it reasonable to round here?*

Since the *estimate* of the area of a curved shape is not precise, it is reasonable to round off the estimate.

Adventure Book - page 34

Page 36

- *Why did Peter and Rosita measure both the area and the length of the foot?*

Students can now apply what Peter said earlier: Although some classmates have the same length or the same area, very few students will have the same length *and* the same area.

Adventure Book - page 36

Adventure Book - page 37

Adventure Book - page 38

Page 37

- *Which of the students could be the "ghost"?*

John and Brian are the most likely candidates although neither of these boys' measurements matches Peter and Rosita's data exactly. This is a good place to discuss the possibilities of measurement error.

- *Why are all the measurements written on the board in whole numbers? Do you think all the students' measurements would have "come out even"? Do you think students rounded the answers?*

Most measurements were probably not whole numbers, but were rounded to the nearest whole number.

Page 38

- *Why did Peter and Rosita decide to follow John?*

The area of the ghost's footprint is within one square centimeter of the area recorded for John's foot, and the length of the ghost's footprint is exactly the same as John's. Also, Rosita noticed that John didn't want to take off his shoes and measure his foot, so she is suspicious of him. (See page 36.)

Journal Prompt

Write a story in which a detective solves a problem by finding the area of a mystery shape.

Homework and Practice

- DPP Bit M provides practice finding area by counting square centimeters. DPP Task N provides addition computation practice.
- For Home Practice Part 4, students solve multiplication problems using square numbers.

Answers for Part 4 of the Home Practice are in the Answer Key at the end of this lesson and at the end of this unit.

Extension

Students trace their footprints on grid paper and find the areas.

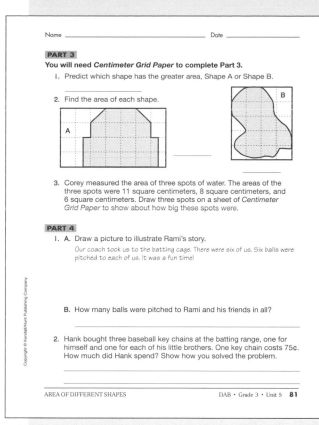

Name _____ Date _____

PART 3
You will need *Centimeter Grid Paper* to complete Part 3.
1. Predict which shape has the greater area, Shape A or Shape B.
   _____
2. Find the area of each shape.

3. Corey measured the area of three spots of water. The areas of the three spots were 11 square centimeters, 8 square centimeters, and 6 square centimeters. Draw three spots on a sheet of *Centimeter Grid Paper* to show about how big these spots were.

PART 4
1. A. Draw a picture to illustrate Rami's story.
      Our coach took us to the batting cage. There were six of us. Six balls were pitched to each of us. It was a fun time!

   B. How many balls were pitched to Rami and his friends in all?
      _____

2. Hank bought three baseball key chains at the batting range, one for himself and one for each of his little brothers. One key chain costs 75¢. How much did Hank spend? Show how you solved the problem.
   _____

AREA OF DIFFERENT SHAPES   DAB · Grade 3 · Unit 5   **81**

Discovery Assignment Book - page 81 (Answers on p. 66)

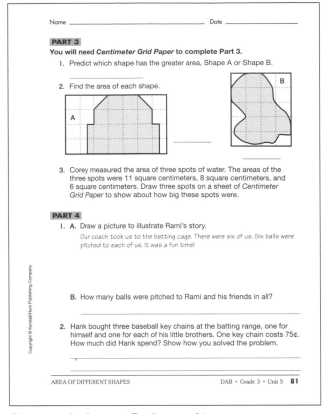

Discovery Assignment Book - page 81

Discovery Assignment Book (p. 81)

Home Practice*

Part 4

I. **A.** Pictures will vary.

B. $6 \times 6 = 36$ balls

2. Solution strategies will vary.
$75¢ \times 3 = 50 + 25 + 50 + 25 + 50 + 25$
$= \$2.25$

---

*Answers for all the Home Practice in the *Discovery Assignment Book* are at the end of the unit.

Lesson 5

Joe the Goldfish

Lesson Overview

Students work in pairs or groups to determine the amount of material it would take to make a raincoat for Joe the Goldfish. They must first design the coat and then determine its area in square centimeters. Students use the Student Rubric: *Solving* to guide their work.

Key Content

- Measuring area by counting square centimeters.
- Solving a problem involving area.
- Solving open-response problems and communicating solution strategies.

Math Facts

DPP items O and P provide practice with math facts.

Assessment

1. Use the *Observational Assessment Record* to document students' abilities to solve open-response problems and communicate solution strategies.
2. Use the Unit 5 *Observational Assessment Record* to update students' *Individual Assessment Record Sheets.*

Curriculum Sequence

Before This Unit

Using Student Rubrics

Students were introduced to the Student Rubric: *Knowing* in Grade 3 Unit 2 Lesson 6 *Spinning Differences*. They used the rubric as a guide for writing about their solution strategies for an open-response problem.

After This Unit

Using Student Rubrics

The Student Rubric: *Telling* will be introduced in Unit 7 Lesson 2 *Katie's Job*.

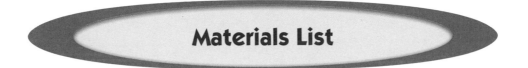

Materials List

Supplies and Copies

Student	Teacher
Supplies for Each Student Group • scissors	**Supplies**
Copies • 1 copy of *A Raincoat for Joe the Goldfish* per student (*Unit Resource Guide* Page 75) • 1 copy of *Centimeter Grid Paper* per student group (*Unit Resource Guide* Page 28)	**Copies/Transparencies** • 1 transparency of *A Raincoat for Joe the Goldfish*, optional (*Unit Resource Guide* Page 75) • 1 transparency of *Centimeter Grid Paper*, optional (*Unit Resource Guide* Page 28)

All blackline masters including assessment, transparency, and DPP masters are also on the Teacher Resource CD.

Student Books

Student Rubrics: *Knowing* and *Solving* (*Student Guide* Appendix A and Appendix B and Inside Back Cover)

Daily Practice and Problems and Home Practice

DPP items O–P (*Unit Resource Guide* Page 19)

Note: Classrooms whose pacing differs significantly from the suggested pacing of the units should use the Math Facts Calendar in Section 4 of the *Facts Resource Guide* to ensure students receive the complete math facts program.

Assessment Tools

Observational Assessment Record (*Unit Resource Guide* Pages 9–10)
Individual Assessment Record Sheet (*Teacher Implementation Guide*, Assessment section)

Daily Practice and Problems

Suggestions for using the DPPs are on page 73.

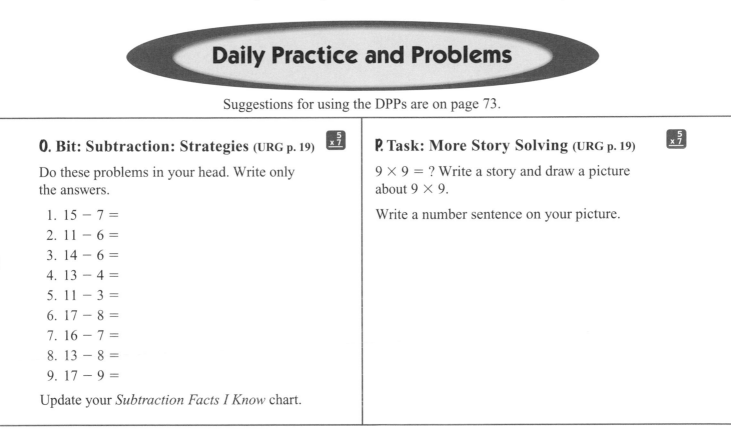

O. Bit: Subtraction: Strategies (URG p. 19) $\boxed{\begin{smallmatrix}5\\ \times\,7\end{smallmatrix}}$

Do these problems in your head. Write only the answers.

1. $15 - 7 =$
2. $11 - 6 =$
3. $14 - 6 =$
4. $13 - 4 =$
5. $11 - 3 =$
6. $17 - 8 =$
7. $16 - 7 =$
8. $13 - 8 =$
9. $17 - 9 =$

Update your *Subtraction Facts I Know* chart.

P. Task: More Story Solving (URG p. 19) $\boxed{\begin{smallmatrix}5\\ \times\,7\end{smallmatrix}}$

$9 \times 9 = ?$ Write a story and draw a picture about 9×9.

Write a number sentence on your picture.

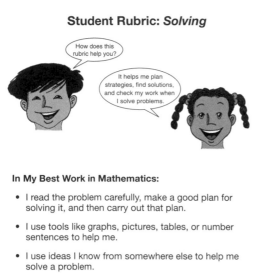

Student Rubric: *Solving*

How does this rubric help you?

It helps me plan strategies, find solutions, and check my work when I solve problems.

In My Best Work in Mathematics:

• I read the problem carefully, make a good plan for solving it, and then carry out that plan.

• I use tools like graphs, pictures, tables, or number sentences to help me.

• I use ideas I know from somewhere else to help me solve a problem.

• I keep working on the problem until I find a good solution.

• I look back at my solution to see if my answer makes sense.

• I look back at my work to see what more I can learn from solving the problem.

Student Guide - Appendix B

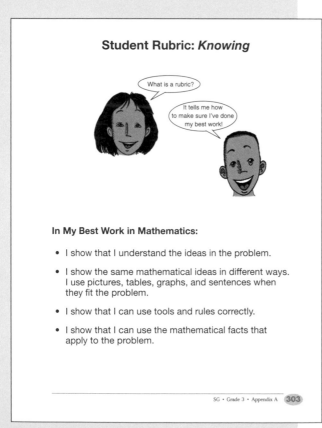

Student Rubric: *Knowing*

What is a rubric?

It tells me how to make sure I've done my best work!

In My Best Work in Mathematics:

• I show that I understand the ideas in the problem.

• I show the same mathematical ideas in different ways. I use pictures, tables, graphs, and sentences when they fit the problem.

• I show that I can use tools and rules correctly.

• I show that I can use the mathematical facts that apply to the problem.

Student Guide - Appendix A

Teaching the Activity

To begin the assessment, present the class with the problem described on the *A Raincoat for Joe the Goldfish* Assessment Blackline Master. Groups of students need to design a raincoat for Joe and determine the area of the raincoat. They will probably have many questions about the design of the raincoat. Should the coat cover Joe's entire body? Should holes be made for the eyes or mouth? What about the fins? The answers to these questions should be left to the discretion of the individual design teams. You may want to point out that even though we can see only one side of Joe in the picture, he has a right side and a left side. You may also want to stress that an important part of this activity is for design team members to work together.

Discuss the *Solving* Student Rubric with students. You might want to post it on a bulletin board so that students will be reminded to use it.

As students solve the problem, check to see whether teams are working well together. You can make anecdotal notations about how individual students are working within a group. After the exercise is done, you can discuss your observations with the groups and compare your notes with the students' journal entries. Also, as they are working, encourage them to use the Student Rubric: *Solving* to guide their work. You may wish to use this activity to review the *Knowing* Student Rubric as well.

When all groups finish, each student should write a description of his or her group's problem-solving process. Afterwards, talk about the criteria outlined in the *Solving* rubric and apply it to several pieces of sample work. (You may wish to use one or both of the rubrics.) Spend time discussing how the work does or does not reflect the defined goals. This kind of discussion helps students learn how to apply the rubric.

Journal Prompt

How did your team work together to design Joe's raincoat and to find the area of the material needed to make the coat? Did each of you have a different job or did you all work together on the whole problem? Did you always agree? If not, how did you settle your differences?

Before you give final scores for the assignment, comment on the first drafts and give students an opportunity to revise their work based on your comments. Remind them, as they revise their work, to use the *Solving* (and *Knowing*) portions of the TIMS Student Rubric as a guide.

Use the following questions to guide your evaluation of students' content knowledge and problem-solving abilities.

Knowing

- Did students use the area of the part of Joe's body covered by the raincoat to find the amount of material needed?
- Did students measure the area accurately?
- Did students correctly compute the area of Joe's body covered by the coat?

Solving

- Did students define the parts of the body the raincoat will cover?
- Did they find a strategy for measuring the area of that part of Joe's body?
- Did they double the measured area of one side to cover both sides of the body?

The samples of student work presented in Figures 8, 9, and 10 show various levels of problem-solving ability and content knowledge. The scores reflect ratings according to our assessment rubrics. The teacher rubrics, and more information about using them, are in the Assessment section of the *Teacher Implementation Guide.*

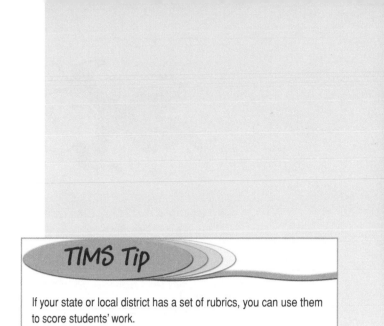

TIMS Tip

If your state or local district has a set of rubrics, you can use them to score students' work.

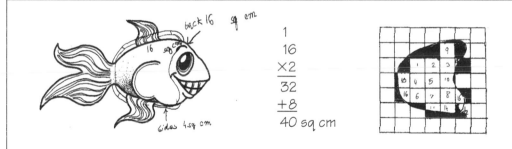

We traced the part of the body where the coat is going to be, we came up with 16 sq cm for the front and the back, the sides and we came up with 4 sq cm and we x it by two and our answer is 40 sq cm for the meterial.

Figure 8: *Pablo communicates his correct answer fairly well*

Knowing, 4

Pablo clearly understood that the problem involved finding the area of the raincoat by counting square centimeters. He counted the square centimeters accurately and used multiplication and addition to compute the total area correctly.

Solving, 4

Pablo identified the elements of the problem correctly: finding the area of the front, back, and sides of the raincoat. He also used a systematic and efficient method for solving the problem.

We measured him in sq. cm. Than we made deasign of Joe's Raincoat and he did 38 sq. cm of material.

Figure 9: *Kelly has difficulty communicating her correct answer*

Knowing, 3
Kelly's diagram shows that she understood she needed to find the area by counting square centimeters, but her measurement is not quite accurate.

Solving, 4
Kelly identified important elements of the problem by designing an appropriate raincoat and by doubling the value of the area she did find.

First I masured it and then I made a raincoat. And Now I am going to masure the raincoat with choklate pieces.

Figure 10: *Ernie has difficulty understanding the problem*

Knowing, 1
Ernie drew a raincoat around Joe and stated that he measured it. However, he did *not* tell us what he measured (length, width, or area), nor did he give the measurement. This response shows that he did not understand the problem's mathematical concepts.

Solving, 2
Ernie's statement that he is planning to cover Joe with "chocolate" pieces indicates that he understood something about how to approach the solution process. However, he was unable to develop an appropriate strategy for solving the problem. (The "chocolate pieces" are the base-ten pieces used in *The TIMS Candy Company* in Unit 4.)

Math Facts

DPP Bit O provides practice with subtraction facts. Task P develops strategies for the multiplication facts (square numbers).

Homework and Practice

Assign the journal prompt that asks students to reflect on their group process of solving the raincoat problem.

Assessment

- Use the *Observational Assessment Record* to document students' abilities to solve open-response problems and communicate solution strategies.

- Transfer appropriate observations from the *Observational Assessment Record* to students' *Individual Assessment Record Sheets*.

At a Glance

Math Facts and Daily Practice and Problems

DPP items O and P practice math facts.

Teaching the Activity

1. Present the problem described on the *A Raincoat for Joe the Goldfish* Assessment Blackline Master.
2. Discuss the Student Rubric: *Solving.*
3. Design team members work together to solve the problem.
4. Encourage teams to use the rubric to guide their work. They may use the *Solving* rubric, the *Knowing* rubric, or both.
5. Students describe their group's problem-solving process.
6. Talk about the criteria outlined in the Student Rubric: *Solving* and apply it to several pieces of sample work. (Review the *Knowing* rubric—optional.)
7. Comment on first drafts and give students an opportunity to revise their work.
8. Score student work on one or both of the rubrics.

Assessment

1. Document students' abilities to solve open-response problems and communicate solution strategies using the *Observational Assessment Record.*
2. Use the Unit 5 *Observational Assessment Record* to update students' *Individual Assessment Record Sheets.*

Answer Key is on page 76.

Notes:

Name _____ Date _____

A Raincoat for
Joe the Goldfish

Joe the Goldfish

Pretend you need to make a raincoat for Joe the Goldfish. Design a raincoat for Joe. Find the area of the raincoat in square centimeters. Use the space below to explain your answer.

Name _____ Date _____

A Raincoat for Joe the Goldfish

Joe the Goldfish

Pretend you need to make a raincoat for Joe the Goldfish. Design a raincoat for Joe. Find the area of the raincoat in square centimeters. Use the space below to explain your answer.

Assessment Blackline Master   URG • Grade 3 • Unit 5 • Lesson 5   75

Unit Resource Guide - page 75

Unit Resource Guide (p. 75)

A Raincoat for Joe the Goldfish*

See Lesson Guide 5 for sample student work scored using the Solving and Knowing dimensions of the *TIMS Multidimensional Rubric*.

*Answers and/or discussion are included in the Lesson Guide.

Using Number Sense at the Book Sale

Estimated Class Sessions	Lesson Overview
1	Students solve a set of word problems involving purchasing books at a bookstore.

Key Content

- Solving multistep word problems involving money.
- Communicating solutions verbally and in writing.

Homework

Assign some or all of the problems for homework.

Materials List

Supplies and Copies

Student	Teacher
Supplies for Each Student	**Supplies**
Copies	**Copies/Transparencies**

All blackline masters including assessment, transparency, and DPP masters are also on the Teacher Resource CD.

Student Books

Using Number Sense at the Book Sale (*Student Guide* Pages 62–64)

Note: Classrooms whose pacing differs significantly from the suggested pacing of the units should use the Math Facts Calendar in Section 4 of the *Facts Resource Guide* to ensure students receive the complete math facts program.

Teaching the Activity

Students can work on these problems individually, in pairs, or in groups. They can complete them all at once or you can distribute them throughout the unit. Create additional problems as needed or encourage students to write their own.

Homework and Practice

Assign some or all of the problems for homework.

Extension

Ask students to write their own problems involving changing money either at a bookstore or a different type of store. Have them swap problems with a partner. After students solve their partners' problems, they can check each other's solutions and strategies.

Student Guide - page 62

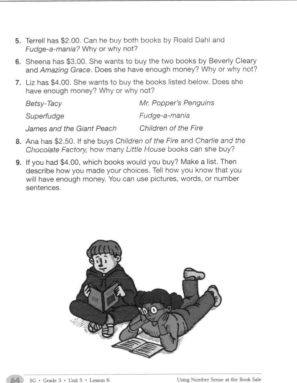

Student Guide - page 63 (Answers on p. 81)

Student Guide - page 64 (Answers on p. 81)

At a Glance

Teaching the Activity

1. Students solve the problems on the *Using Number Sense at the Book Sale* Activity Pages in the *Student Guide.*
2. Students discuss their solution strategies with the class.

Homework

Assign some or all of the problems for homework.

Extension

Ask students to write their own problems involving changing money. Students can then exchange the problems to solve.

Answer Key is on page 81.

Notes:

Student Guide (p. 63)

Explanations will vary.

1. **A.** 4 quarters

   B. 1 quarter

2. Yes. One book costs 50¢ and the other is less than 50¢. Altogether the two cost less than one dollar.

3. Yes. One book costs 50¢. The other two, together, cost less than 50¢. All three would cost less than one dollar.

4. No. The two books cost more than $1.25. 95¢ is close to $1 and $45 is a good bit more than 25¢.

Price List

Title	Author	Price
Betsy-Tacy	Maud Hart Lovelace	20¢
Mr. Popper's Penguins	Richard and Florence Atwater	25¢
Ramón Makes a Trade	Barbara Ritchie	45¢
Superfudge	Judy Blume	50¢
Fudge-a-mania	Judy Blume	50¢
Charlie and the Chocolate Factory	Roald Dahl	75¢
James and the Giant Peach	Roald Dahl	75¢
Ramona Quimby, Age 8	Beverly Cleary	95¢
Ramona and Her Father	Beverly Cleary	95¢
Children of the Fire	Harriette Gillem Robinet	$1.00
Amazing Grace	Mary Hoffman	$1.50
Little House Books	Laura Ingalls Wilder	4 for $1.00

1. Pretend you are going to the book store with quarters.
   A. Do you need three or four quarters to buy *Ramona Quimby, Age 8*?
   B. How many quarters do you need to buy *Betsy-Tacy*?

2. Susie has $1.00. Can she buy *Ramón Makes a Trade* and *Superfudge*? Why or why not?

3. James has $1.00. Can he buy *Betsy-Tacy*, *Mr. Popper's Penguins*, and *Fudge-a-mania*? Why or why not?

4. Tino has $1.25. Does he have enough money to buy *Ramón Makes a Trade* and *Ramona and Her Father*? Why or why not?

Using Number Sense at the Book Sale   SG • Grade 3 • Unit 5 • Lesson 6   **63**

Student Guide - page 63

Student Guide (p. 64)

5. Yes. The two books by Dahl cost 75¢ each or $1.50. Since *Fudge-a-mania* costs 50¢, Terrell has enough money.

6. No. The two books by Beverly Cleary cost about $2.00. *Amazing Grace* costs a lot more than $1.00. All three will cost more than $3.00.

7. Yes. *Superfudge, Fudge-a-mania,* and *Children of the Fire* together cost $2.00. *James and the Giant Peach* and *Mr. Popper's Penguins* cost an additional $1.00. So far the cost is $3.00. After adding on *Betsy-Tacy,* the total is $3.20.

8. Three *Little House* books; *Children of the Fire* and *Charlie and the Chocolate Factory* together cost $1.75. Counting up: $1.75 to $2.00 is 25¢; $2.00 to $2.50 is 50¢ more. Ana has 75¢ to spend. If four books cost $1.00, one costs 25¢. Ana can purchase three.

9. Answers will vary.

5. Terrell has $2.00. Can he buy both books by Roald Dahl and *Fudge-a-mania*? Why or why not?

6. Sheena has $3.00. She wants to buy the two books by Beverly Cleary and *Amazing Grace*. Does she have enough money? Why or why not?

7. Liz has $4.00. She wants to buy the books listed below. Does she have enough money? Why or why not?

Betsy-Tacy	*Mr. Popper's Penguins*
Superfudge	*Fudge-a-mania*
James and the Giant Peach	*Children of the Fire*

8. Ana has $2.50. If she buys *Children of the Fire* and *Charlie and the Chocolate Factory,* how many *Little House* books can she buy?

9. If you had $4.00, which books would you buy? Make a list. Then describe how you made your choices. Tell how you know that you will have enough money. You can use pictures, words, or number sentences.

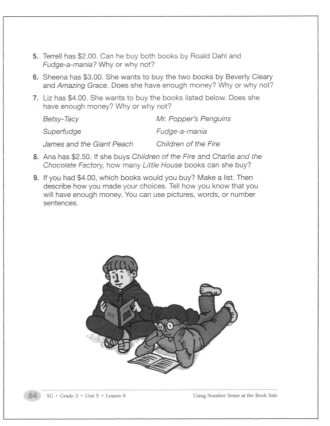

64   SG • Grade 3 • Unit 5 • Lesson 6   Using Number Sense at the Book Sale

Student Guide - page 64

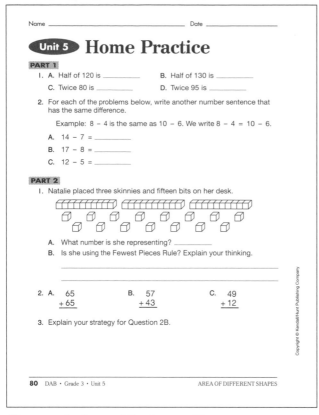

Discovery Assignment Book - page 80

Discovery Assignment Book (p. 80)

Part 1

1. **A.** 60   **B.** 65

    C. 160   **D.** 190

2. Answers will vary.

    A. $15 - 8$ **B.** $19 - 10$ **C.** $10 - 3$

Part 2

1. **A.** 45

    B. No. She could trade 10 bits for 1 skinny. She would then have 4 skinnies and 5 bits.

2. **A.** 130   **B.** 100   **C.** 61

3. Strategies will vary. Possible response: $50 + 40 + 10 = 100$

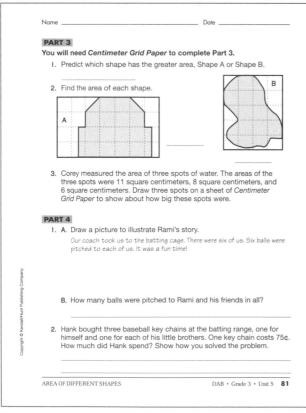

Discovery Assignment Book - page 81

Discovery Assignment Book (p. 81)

Part 3

1. Answers will vary.

2. Shape A is about 17 sq cm. Shape B is about 13 sq cm.

3. Shapes will vary. Area of the spots should be 11 sq cm, 8 sq cm, and 6 sq cm. Accept a spot with square corners but discuss the likelihood that spreading water would form this type of shape. Compare students' "spots."

Part 4

1. **A.** Pictures will vary.

    B. $6 \times 6 = 36$ balls

2. Solution strategies will vary; $75¢ \times 3 = 50 + 25 + 50 + 25 + 50 + 25 = \$2.25$

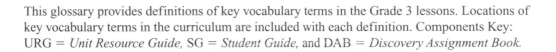

Glossary

This glossary provides definitions of key vocabulary terms in the Grade 3 lessons. Locations of key vocabulary terms in the curriculum are included with each definition. Components Key: URG = *Unit Resource Guide,* SG = *Student Guide,* and DAB = *Discovery Assignment Book.*

A

Area (URG Unit 5; SG Unit 5)
The area of a shape is the amount of space it covers, measured in square units.

Array (URG Unit 7 & Unit 11)
An array is an arrangement of elements into a rectangular pattern of (horizontal) rows and (vertical) columns. (*See* column and row.)

Associative Property of Addition (URG Unit 2)
For any three numbers a, b, and c we have $a + (b + c) = (a + b) + c$. For example in finding the sum of 4, 8, and 2, one can compute $4 + 8$ first and then add 2: $(4 + 8) + 2 = 14$. Alternatively, we can compute $8 + 2$ and then add the result to 4: $4 + (8 + 2) = 4 + 10 = 14$.

Average (URG Unit 5)
A number that can be used to represent a typical value in a set of data. (*See also* mean and median.)

Axes (URG Unit 8; SG Unit 8)
Reference lines on a graph. In the Cartesian coordinate system, the axes are two perpendicular lines that meet at the origin. The singular of axes is axis.

B

Base (of a cube model) (URG Unit 18; SG Unit 18)
The part of a cube model that sits on the "ground."

Base-Ten Board (URG Unit 4)
A tool to help children organize base-ten pieces when they are representing numbers.

Base-Ten Pieces (URG Unit 4; SG Unit 4)
A set of manipulatives used to model our number system as shown in the figure at the right. Note that a skinny is made of 10 bits, a flat is made of 100 bits, and a pack is made of 1000 bits.

Base-Ten Shorthand (SG Unit 4)
A pictorial representation of the base-ten pieces as shown.

Nickname	Picture	Shorthand
bit	□	•
skinny	▭▭▭▭▭▭▭▭	/
flat	▦	▱
pack	▦	▱

Best-Fit Line (URG Unit 9; SG Unit 9; DAB Unit 9)
The line that comes closest to the most number of points on a point graph.

Bit (URG Unit 4; SG Unit 4)
A cube that measures 1 cm on each edge. It is the smallest of the base-ten pieces that is often used to represent 1. (*See also* base-ten pieces.)

C

Capacity (URG Unit 16)
1. The volume of the inside of a container.
2. The largest volume a container can hold.

Cartesian Coordinate System (URG Unit 8)
A method of locating points on a flat surface by means of numbers. This method is named after its originator, René Descartes. (*See also* coordinates.)

Centimeter (cm)
A unit of measure in the metric system equal to one-hundredth of a meter. (1 inch = 2.54 cm)

Column (URG Unit 11)
In an array, the objects lined up vertically.

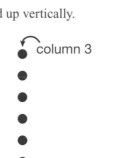
column 3

Common Fraction (URG Unit 15)
Any fraction that is written with a numerator and denominator that are whole numbers. For example, $\frac{3}{4}$ and $\frac{9}{4}$ are both common fractions. (*See also* decimal fraction.)

Commutative Property of Addition (URG Unit 2 & Unit 11)
This is also known as the Order Property of Addition. Changing the order of the addends does not change the sum. For example, $3 + 5 = 5 + 3 = 8$. Using variables, $n + m = m + n$.

Commutative Property of Multiplication (URG Unit 11)
Changing the order of the factors in a multiplication problem does not change the result, e.g., $7 \times 3 = 3 \times 7 = 21$. (*See also* turn-around facts.)

Congruent (URG Unit 12 & Unit 17; SG Unit 12)
Figures with the same shape and size.

Convenient Number (URG Unit 6)
A number used in computation that is close enough to give a good estimate, but is also easy to compute mentally, e.g., 25 and 30 are convenient numbers for 27.

Coordinates (URG Unit 8; SG Unit 8)
An ordered pair of numbers that locates points on a flat surface by giving distances from a pair of coordinate axes. For example, if a point has coordinates (4, 5) it is 4 units from the vertical axis and 5 units from the horizontal axis.

Counting Back (URG Unit 2)
A strategy for subtracting in which students start from a larger number and then count down until the number is reached. For example, to solve $8 - 3$, begin with 8 and count down three, 7, 6, 5.

Counting Down (*See* counting back.)

Counting Up (URG Unit 2)
A strategy for subtraction in which the student starts at the lower number and counts on to the higher number. For example, to solve $8 - 5$, the student starts at 5 and counts up three numbers (6, 7, 8). So $8 - 5 = 3$.

Cube (SG Unit 18)
A three-dimensional shape with six congruent square faces.

Cubic Centimeter (cc) (URG Unit 16; SG Unit 16)
The volume of a cube that is one centimeter long on each edge.

1 cm
1 cm
1 cm
cubic centimeter

Cup (URG Unit 16)
A unit of volume equal to 8 fluid ounces, one-half pint.

D

Decimal Fraction (URG Unit 15)
A fraction written as a decimal. For example, 0.75 and 0.4 are decimal fractions and $\frac{75}{100}$ and $\frac{4}{10}$ are called common fractions. (*See also* fraction.)

Denominator (URG Unit 13)
The number below the line in a fraction. The denominator indicates the number of equal parts in which the unit whole is divided. For example, the 5 is the denominator in the fraction $\frac{2}{5}$. In this case the unit whole is divided into five equal parts.

Density (URG Unit 16)
The ratio of an object's mass to its volume.

Difference (URG Unit 2)
The answer to a subtraction problem.

Dissection (URG Unit 12 & Unit 17)
Cutting or decomposing a geometric shape into smaller shapes that cover it exactly.

Distributive Property of Multiplication over Addition (URG Unit 19)
For any three numbers $a, b,$ and $c, a \times (b + c) = a \times b + a \times c$. The distributive property is the foundation for most methods of multidigit multiplication. For example, $9 \times (17) = 9 \times (10 + 7) = 9 \times 10 + 9 \times 7 = 90 + 63 = 153$.

E

Equal-Arm Balance
See two-pan balance.

Equilateral Triangle (URG Unit 7)
A triangle with all sides of equal length and all angles of equal measure.

Equivalent Fractions (SG Unit 17)
Fractions that have the same value, e.g., $\frac{2}{4} = \frac{1}{2}$.

Estimate (URG Unit 5 & Unit 6)
1. (verb) To find *about* how many.
2. (noun) An approximate number.

Extrapolation (URG Unit 7)
Using patterns in data to make predictions or to estimate values that lie beyond the range of values in the set of data.

F

Fact Family (URG Unit 11; SG Unit 11)
Related math facts, e.g., $3 \times 4 = 12$, $4 \times 3 = 12$, $12 \div 3 = 4$, $12 \div 4 = 3$.

Factor (URG Unit 11; SG Unit 11)
1. In a multiplication problem, the numbers that are multiplied together. In the problem $3 \times 4 = 12$, 3 and 4 are the factors.
2. Whole numbers that can be multiplied together to get a number. That is, numbers that divide a number evenly, e.g., 1, 2, 3, 4, 6, and 12 are all the factors of 12.

Fewest Pieces Rule (URG Unit 4 & Unit 6; SG Unit 4)
Using the least number of base-ten pieces to represent a number. (*See also* base-ten pieces.)

Flat (URG Unit 4; SG Unit 4)
A block that measures 1 cm $\times$ 10 cm $\times$ 10 cm. It is one of the base-ten pieces that is often used to represent 100. (*See also* base-ten pieces.)

Flip (URG Unit 12)
A motion of the plane in which a figure is reflected over a line so that any point and its image are the same distance from the line.

Fraction (URG Unit 15)
A number that can be written as $\frac{a}{b}$ where a and b are whole numbers and b is not zero. For example, $\frac{1}{2}$, 0.5, and 2 are all fractions since 0.5 can be written as $\frac{5}{10}$ and 2 can be written as $\frac{2}{1}$.

Front-End Estimation (URG Unit 6)
Estimation by looking at the left-most digit.

G

Gallon (gal) (URG Unit 16)
A unit of volume equal to four quarts.

Gram
The basic unit used to measure mass.

H

Hexagon (SG Unit 12)
A six-sided polygon.

Horizontal Axis (SG Unit 1)
In a coordinate grid, the *x*-axis. The axis that extends from left to right.

I

Interpolation (URG Unit 7)
Making predictions or estimating values that lie between data points in a set of data.

J

K

Kilogram
1000 grams.

L

Likely Event (SG Unit 1)
An event that has a high probability of occurring.

Line of Symmetry (URG Unit 12)
A line is a line of symmetry for a plane figure if, when the figure is folded along this line, the two parts match exactly.

Line Symmetry (URG Unit 12; SG Unit 12)
A figure has line symmetry if it has at least one line of symmetry.

Liter (l) (URG Unit 16; SG Unit 16)
Metric unit used to measure volume. A liter is a little more than a quart.

M

Magic Square (URG Unit 2)
A square array of digits in which the sums of the rows, columns, and main diagonals are the same.

Making a Ten (URG Unit 2)
Strategies for addition and subtraction that make use of knowing the sums to ten. For example, knowing $6 + 4 = 10$ can be helpful in finding $10 - 6 = 4$ and $11 - 6 = 5$.

Mass (URG Unit 9 & Unit 16; SG Unit 9)
The amount of matter in an object.

Mean (URG Unit 5)
An average of a set of numbers that is found by adding the values of the data and dividing by the number of values.

Measurement Division (URG Unit 7)
Division as equal grouping. The total number of objects and the number of objects in each group are known. The number of groups is the unknown. For example, tulip bulbs come in packages of 8. If 216 bulbs are sold, how many packages are sold?

Measurement Error (URG Unit 9)
The unavoidable error that occurs due to the limitations inherent to any measurement instrument.

Median (URG Unit 5; DAB Unit 5)
For a set with an odd number of data arranged in order, it is the middle number. For an even number of data arranged in order, it is the number halfway between the two middle numbers.

Meniscus (URG Unit 16; SG Unit 16)
The curved surface formed when a liquid creeps up the side of a container (for example, a graduated cylinder).

Meter (m)
The standard unit of length measure in the metric system. One meter is approximately 39 inches.

Milliliter (ml) (URG Unit 16; SG Unit 16)
A measure of capacity in the metric system that is the volume of a cube that is one centimeter long on each edge.

Multiple (URG Unit 3 & Unit 11)
A number is a multiple of another number if it is evenly divisible by that number. For example, 12 is a multiple of 2 since 2 divides 12 evenly.

N

Numerator (URG Unit 13)
The number written above the line in a fraction. For example, the 2 is the numerator in the fraction $\frac{2}{5}$. (*See also* denominator.)

O

One-Dimensional Object (URG Unit 18; SG Unit 18)
An object is one-dimensional if it is made up of pieces of lines and curves.

Ordered Pairs (URG Unit 8)
A pair of numbers that gives the coordinates of a point on a grid in relation to the origin. The horizontal coordinate is given first; the vertical coordinate is given second. For example, the ordered pair (5, 3) tells us to move five units to the right of the origin and 3 units up.

Origin (URG Unit 8)
The point at which the *x*- and *y*-axes (horizontal and vertical axes) intersect on a coordinate plane. The origin is described by the ordered pair (0, 0) and serves as a reference point so that all the points on the plane can be located by ordered pairs.

P

Pack (URG Unit 4; SG Unit 4)
A cube that measures 10 cm on each edge. It is one of the base-ten pieces that is often used to represent 1000. (*See also* base-ten pieces.)

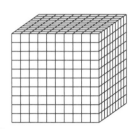

Palindrome (URG Unit 6)
A number, word, or phrase that reads the same forward and backward, e.g., 12321.

Parallel Lines (URG Unit 18)
Lines that are in the same direction. In the plane, parallel lines are lines that do not intersect.

Parallelogram (URG Unit 18)
A quadrilateral with two pairs of parallel sides.

Partitive Division (URG Unit 7)
Division as equal sharing. The total number of objects and the number of groups are known. The number of objects in each group is the unknown. For example, Frank has 144 marbles that he divides equally into 6 groups. How many marbles are in each group?

Pentagon (SG Unit 12)
A five-sided, five-angled polygon.

Perimeter (URG Unit 7; DAB Unit 7)
The distance around a two-dimensional shape.

Pint (URG Unit 16)
A unit of volume measure equal to 16 fluid ounces, i.e., two cups.

Polygon
A two-dimensional connected figure made of line segments in which each endpoint of every side meets with an endpoint of exactly one other side.

Population (URG Unit 1; SG Unit 1)
A collection of persons or things whose properties will be analyzed in a survey or experiment.

Prediction (SG Unit 1)
Using data to declare or foretell what is likely to occur.

Prime Number (URG Unit 11)
A number that has exactly two factors. For example, 7 has exactly two distinct factors, 1 and 7.

Prism
A three-dimensional figure that has two congruent faces, called bases, that are parallel to each other, and all other faces are parallelograms.

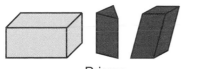

Prisms   Not a prism

Product (URG Unit 11; SG Unit 11; DAB Unit 11)
The answer to a multiplication problem. In the problem $3 \times 4 = 12$, 12 is the product.

Q

Quadrilateral (URG Unit 18)
A polygon with four sides.

Quart (URG Unit 16)
A unit of volume equal to 32 fluid ounces; one quarter of a gallon.

R

Recording Sheet (URG Unit 4)
A place value chart used for addition and subtraction problems.

Rectangular Prism (URG Unit 18; SG Unit 18)
A prism whose bases are rectangles. A right rectangular prism is a prism having all faces rectangles.

Regular (URG Unit 7; DAB Unit 7)
A polygon is regular if all sides are of equal length and all angles are equal.

Remainder (URG Unit 7)
Something that remains or is left after a division problem. The portion of the dividend that is not evenly divisible by the divisor, e.g., $16 \div 5 = 3$ with 1 as a remainder.

Right Angle (SG Unit 12)
An angle that measures 90°.

Rotation (turn) (URG Unit 12)
A transformation (motion) in which a figure is turned a specified angle and direction around a point.

Row (URG Unit 11)
In an array, the objects lined up horizontally.

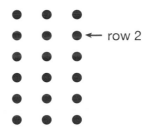

Rubric (URG Unit 2)
A written guideline for assigning scores to student work, for the purpose of assessment.

S

Sample (URG Unit 1; SG Unit 1)
A part or subset of a population.

Skinny (URG Unit 4; SG Unit 4)
A block that measures 1 cm $\times$ 1 cm $\times$ 10 cm. It is one of the base-ten pieces that is often used to represent 10. (*See also* base-ten pieces.)

Square Centimeter (sq cm) (SG Unit 5)
The area of a square that is 1 cm long on each side.

Square Number (SG Unit 11)
A number that is the product of a whole number multiplied by itself. For example, 25 is a square number since $5 \times 5 = 25$. A square number can be represented by a square array with the same number of rows as columns. A square array for 25 has 5 rows of 5 objects in each row or 25 total objects.

Standard Masses
A set of objects with convenient masses, usually 1 g, 10 g, 100 g, etc.

Sum (URG Unit 2; SG Unit 2)
The answer to an addition problem.

Survey (URG Unit 14; SG Unit 14)
An investigation conducted by collecting data from a sample of a population and then analyzing it. Usually surveys are used to make predictions about the entire population.

T

Tangrams (SG Unit 12)
A type of geometric puzzle. A shape is given and it must be covered exactly with seven standard shapes called tans.

Thinking Addition (URG Unit 2)
A strategy for subtraction that uses a related addition problem. For example, $15 - 7 = 8$ because $8 + 7 = 15$.

Three-Dimensional (URG Unit 18; SG Unit 18)
Existing in three-dimensional space; having length, width, and depth.

TIMS Laboratory Method (URG Unit 1; SG Unit 1)
A method that students use to organize experiments and investigations. It involves four components: draw, collect, graph, and explore. It is a way to help students learn about the scientific method.

Turn (URG Unit 12)
(*See* rotation.)

Turn-Around Facts (URG Unit 2 & Unit 11 p. 37; SG Unit 11)
Addition facts that have the same addends but in a different order, e.g., $3 + 4 = 7$ and $4 + 3 = 7$. (*See also* commutative property of addition and commutative property of multiplication.)

Two-Dimensional (URG Unit 18; SG Unit 18)
Existing in the plane; having length and width.

Two-Pan Balance
A device for measuring the mass of an object by balancing the object against a number of standard masses (usually multiples of 1 unit, 10 units, and 100 units, etc.).

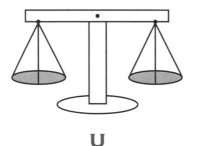

U

Unit (of measurement) (URG Unit 18)
A precisely fixed quantity used to measure. For example, centimeter, foot, kilogram, and quart are units of measurement.

Using a Ten (URG Unit 2)
1. A strategy for addition that uses partitions of the number 10. For example, one can find $8 + 6$ by thinking $8 + 6 = 8 + 2 + 4 = 10 + 4 = 14$.
2. A strategy for subtraction that uses facts that involve subtracting 10. For example, students can use $17 - 10 = 7$ to learn the "close fact" $17 - 9 = 8$.

Using Doubles (URG Unit 2)
Strategies for addition and subtraction that use knowing doubles. For example, one can find $7 + 8$ by thinking $7 + 8 = 7 + 7 + 1 = 14 + 1 = 15$. Knowing $7 + 7 = 14$ can be helpful in finding $14 - 7 = 7$ and $14 - 8 = 6$.

V

Value (URG Unit 1; SG Unit 1)
The possible outcomes of a variable. For example, red, green, and blue are possible values for the variable *color.* Two meters and 1.65 meters are possible values for the variable *length.*

Variable (URG Unit 1; SG Unit 1)
1. An attribute or quantity that changes or varies.
2. A symbol that can stand for a variable.

Vertex (URG Unit 12; SG Unit 12)
1. A point where the sides of a polygon meet.
2. A point where the edges of a three-dimensional object meet.

Vertical Axis (SG Unit 1)
In a coordinate grid, the y-axis. It is perpendicular to the horizontal axis.

Volume (URG Unit 16; SG Unit 16)
The measure of the amount of space occupied by an object.

Volume by Displacement (URG Unit 16)
A way of measuring volume of an object by measuring the amount of water (or some other fluid) it displaces.

W

Weight (URG Unit 9)
A measure of the pull of gravity on an object. One unit for measuring weight is the pound.

X

Y

Z